A Pam Schiller Book and CD

Wild, Wild West

CD INSIDE!

26 Songs and Over 300 Activities for Young Children

Pam Schiller

Gryphon House, Inc.
Beltsville, Maryland

Bulk purchase

Gryphon House books are available for special premiums and sales promotions as well as for fund-raising use. Special editions or book excerpts also can be created to specification. For details, contact the Marketing Director at Gryphon House.

Wild, Wild West

© 2006 Pam Schiller
Printed in the United States of America.

Illustrations: Deborah Johnson
Cover Art: © 2002 Getty Images, Inc. gettyimages.com

Published by Gryphon House, Inc.
10726 Tucker Street, Beltsville, MD 20705
301.595.9500; 301.595.0051 (fax); 800.638.0928 (toll-free)

Visit us on the web at www.ghbooks.com

 Gryphon House is a member of the Green Press Initiative, a nonprofit program dedicated to supporting publishers in their efforts to reduce their use of fiber sourced forests. For further information visit www.greenpressinitiative.org

Library of Congress Cataloging-in-Publication Data

Schiller, Pamela Byrne.
  Wild, wild west / Pam Schiller and Richele Bartkowiak ; illustrations, Deborah Wright.
     p. cm.
  Includes bibliographical references and index.
  ISBN-13: 978-0-87659-043-0
  ISBN-10: 0-87659-043-1
 1. Language arts (Early childhood)--Activity programs. 2. Children's songs. 3. Early childhood education--Activity programs. I. Bartkowiak, Richele. II. Wright, Deborah, ill. III. Title.
  LB1139.5.L35S357 2006
   372.87--dc22

                               2006004449

Wild, Wild West

Pam Schiller

Special Needs Adaptations by Clarissa Willis

Acknowledgments

I would like to thank the following people for their contributions to this book. The special needs adaptations were written by Clarissa Willis. The

Clarissa Willis   Patrick Brennan   Richele Bartkowiak

CD is arranged by Patrick Brennan, and performed by Richele Bartkowiak and Patrick Brennan. It was engineered and mixed by Jeff Smith at Southwest Recordings. —Pam Schiller

Books written by Pam Schiller

The Bilingual Book of Rhymes, Songs, Stories, and Fingerplays, with Rafael Lara-Alecio and Beverly J. Irby

The Complete Book of Activities, Games, Stories, Props, Recipes, and Dances, with Jackie Silberg

The Complete Book of Rhymes, Songs, Poems, Fingerplays, and Chants, with Jackie Silberg

The Complete Daily Curriculum for Early Childhood: Over 1200 Easy Activities to Support Multiple Intelligences and Learning Styles, with Pat Phipps

The Complete Resource Book: An Early Childhood Curriculum, with Kay Hastings

The Complete Resource Book for Infants: Over 700 Experiences for Children From Birth to 18 Months

The Complete Resource Book for Toddlers and Twos: Over 2000 Experiences and Ideas

Count on Math: Activities for Small Hands and Lively Minds, with Lynne Peterson

Creating Readers: Over 1000 Games, Activities, Tongue Twisters, Fingerplays, Songs, and Stories to Get Children Excited About Reading

Do You Know the Muffin Man?, with Thomas Moore

The Instant Curriculum, Revised, with Joan Rosanno

The Practical Guide to Quality Child Care, with Patricia Carter Dyke

Start Smart: Building Brain Power in the Early Years

The Values Book, with Tamera Bryant

Where Is Thumbkin?, with Thomas Moore

Table of Contents

Before serving food to children, be aware of children's food allergies and sensitivities, as well as any religious or cultural practices that exclude certain foods. Be sure to incorporate this information into your daily planning.

Introduction

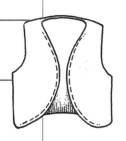

Music in the Early Years

Music is a universal language, and singing is a hallmark of the early childhood classroom. Children love to sing! Teachers love to sing! Age makes no difference. Culture makes no difference.

Singing songs enriches thematic content, supports literacy concepts, and optimizes memory and learning. When you extend classroom activities, including modifications for special needs and English language learner populations, it is a perfect package. *Wild, Wild West* is one of eight thematic book/CD sets that offer all of these resources in one package.

Thematic Content

Wild, Wild West overlaps several typical early childhood themes: Cowboys and Cowgirls, Prairie Life, Animals, Manners, and Rodeo Time. Read the lyrics and decide the best fit in your curriculum for each song.

Each song is accompanied by a list of facts titled "Did You Know?" These facts provide background information about the song, interesting facts about the topic or lyrics, historical information, or some form of trivia you might use as a springboard to discussion. This feature will save you hours of research and adds significantly to the value of the song.

Literacy Concepts

Young children need experiences that allow them to develop and practice basic literacy skills, such as listening, oral language development, phonological awareness, letter knowledge, print awareness, and comprehension. Suggestions for using the songs in *Wild, Wild West* as a springboard for teaching these literacy skills accompany every title. Below is a definition of each literacy skill and the sub-skills they encompass.

○ **Listening:** the development of age-appropriate attention span, as well as the ability to listen for a variety of purposes; for example, details, directions, and sounds.

○ **Oral Language Development:** the acquisition of vocabulary, the fine-tuning of grammar, and the increase in sentence length and complexity.

○ **Phonological Awareness:** sensitivity to the sounds of language. Phonological awareness begins with babbling and cooing and goes all the way through the understanding of sound and symbol relationships and decoding. The skills in the higher end of the phonological awareness continuum—sound and symbol relationship and decoding—are appropriate for children who are age five or older.

○ **Segmentation:** the breaking apart of words by syllable or letter; for example, children clap the breaks in the word di-no-saur.

○ **Rhyme:** words that sound alike. The ending sound of the words is the same, but the initial consonant sound is different, for example, cat and hat or rake and cake.

○ **Alliteration:** the repetition of a consonant sound in a series of words; for example, Peter Piper picked a peck of pickled peppers. Children need to be able to hear the repetition of the /p/ sound, but do not need to identify that the sound is made by the letter "p".

○ **Onomatopoeia:** words that imitate the sound they are describing; for example, *pitter-patter, moo, quack, beep,* and so on.

○ **Letter Knowledge:** the visual recognition of each letter of the alphabet, both lowercase and uppercase.

○ **Print Awareness:** the understanding that print has many functions; for example, telling a story, making a list, as part of signs, in news articles, in recipes, and so on. It is also the awareness that print moves left to right and top to bottom.

○ **Comprehension:** the internalization of a story or a concept.

Optimizing Memory and Learning

Singing boosts memory and keeps the brain alert. Increased memory and alertness optimize the potential for learning. When we sing we generally feel good. That sense of well-being causes the brain to release endorphins into the blood stream and those endorphins act as a memory fixative. When we sing we automatically increase our oxygen intake, which, in turn, increases our alertness. Scientific research has validated what early childhood professionals know intuitively—that singing has a positive effect on learning.

Expanding Children's Learning With Activities

Using songs as a springboard for activities is a good way to bring the lyrics of the song into a meaningful context for children. Dressing like a cowboy after singing "Tiny Cowboy Joe" reinforces and creates meaningful context for the specific characteristics of western life. Exploring face paint, designing smiley faces, roping a cow, having your jumps timed by a stop watch, playing a barrel race game, and eating rodeo treats after singing "The Rodeo" helps children better understand the characteristics of the rodeo, as well as the role clowns and riders play in the event. Reading a book about the rodeo after singing about the rodeo also helps expand children's understanding. Literature selections are provided for each song. Integrating the teaching of themes and skills with songs, literature, and multidisciplinary activities provides a comprehensive approach for helping children recognize the patterns and the interconnected relationships of what they are learning.

Throughout the book, questions to ask children appear in italics. These questions are intended to help children think and reflect on what they have learned. This reflective process optimizes the opportunity for children to apply the information and experiences they have encountered.

Modifications

Suggestions for children with special needs and suggestions for English language learners accompany the song activities when appropriate. These features allow teachers to use the activities with diverse populations. All children love to sing and the benefits apply to all!

Special Needs

The inclusion of children with disabilities in preschool and child care programs is increasingly common. Parents, teachers, and researchers have found that children benefit in many ways from integrated programs that are designed to meet the needs of all children. Many children with disabilities, however, need accommodations to participate successfully in the general classroom.

Included in the extensions and activities for each song are adaptations for children with special needs. These adaptations allow all children to experience the song and related activities in a way that will maximize their learning opportunities. The adaptations are specifically for children who have needs in the following areas:

○ sensory integration
○ distractibility
○ hearing loss
○ spatial organization
○ language, receptive and expressive
○ fine motor coordination
○ cognitive challenges

The following general strategies from Kathleen Bulloch (2003) are for children who have difficulty listening and speaking.

Difficulty	Adaptations/Modifications/Strategies
Listening	○ State the objective—provide a reason for listening ○ Use a photo card ○ Give explanations in small, discrete steps ○ Be concise with verbal information: "Evan, please sit," instead of "Evan, would you please sit down in your chair?" ○ Provide visuals ○ Have the child repeat directions ○ Have the child close his eyes and try to visualize the information ○ Provide manipulative tasks ○ When giving directions to the class, leave a pause between each step so the child can carry out the process in her mind ○ Shorten the listening time required ○ Pre-teach difficult vocabulary and concepts
Verbal Expression	○ Provide a prompt, such as beginning the sentence for the child or giving a picture cue ○ Accept an alternate form of information-sharing, such as artistic creation, photos, charade or pantomime, and demonstration ○ Ask questions that require short answers ○ Specifically teach body and language expression ○ First ask questions at the information level—giving facts and asking for facts back ○ Wait for children to respond; don't call on the first child to raise his hand ○ Have the child break in gradually by speaking in smaller groups and then in larger groups

English Language Learners

Strategies for English language learners are also provided to maximize their learning potential.

The following are general strategies for working with English language learners (Gray, Fleischman, 2004-05):

- **Keep the language simple.** Speak simply and clearly. Use short, complete sentences in a normal tone of voice. Avoid using slang, idioms, or figures of speech.
- **Use actions and illustrations to reinforce oral statements.** Appropriate prompts and facial expressions help convey meaning.
- **Ask for completion, not generation.** Ask children to choose answers from a list or to complete a partially finished sentence. Encourage children to use language as much as possible to gain confidence over time.
- **Model correct usage and judiciously correct errors.** Use corrections to positively reinforce children's use of English. When English language learners make a mistake or use awkward language, they are often attempting to apply what they know about their first language to English. For example, a Spanish-speaking child may say, "It fell from me," a direct translation from Spanish, instead of "I dropped it."
- **Use visual aids.** Present classroom content and information in a way that engages children—by using graphic organizers (word web, story maps, KWL charts), photographs, concrete materials, and graphs, for example.

Involving English Language Learners in Music Activities

Music is a universal language that draws people together. For English language learners, music can be a powerful vehicle for language learning and community-building. Music and singing are important to second language learners for many reasons, including:

- The rhythms of music help children hear the sounds and intonation patterns of a new language.
- Musical lyrics and accompanying motions help children learn new vocabulary.
- Repetitive patterns of language in songs help children internalize the sentence structure of English.
- Important cultural information is conveyed to young children in the themes of songs.

Strategies for involving English language learners in music activities vary according to the children's level of proficiency in the English language.

Level of Proficiency	Strategies
Beginning English Language Learners	<ul><li>Keep the child near you and model motions as you engage in group singing.</li><li>Use hand gestures, movements, and signs as often as possible to accompany song lyrics, making sure to tie a specific motion to a specific word.</li><li>Refer to real objects in the environment that are named in a song.</li><li>Stress the intonation, sounds, and patterns in language by speaking the lyrics of the song while performing actions or referring to objects in the environment.</li><li>Use simple, more common vocabulary. For example, use round instead of circular.</li></ul>
Intermediate-Level English Language Learners	<ul><li>Say the song before singing it, so children can hear the words and rhythms of the lyrics.</li><li>Use motions, gestures, and signs to help children internalize the meaning of song lyrics. Be sure the motion is tied clearly to the associated word.</li><li>Throughout the day, repeat the language patterns found in songs in various activities.</li><li>Stress the language patterns in songs, and pause as children fill in the blanks.</li><li>Adapt the patterns of song, using familiar vocabulary.</li></ul>
Advanced English Language Learners	<ul><li>Use visuals to cue parts of a song.</li><li>Use graphic organizers to introduce unfamiliar information.</li><li>Use synonyms for words heard in songs to expand children's vocabulary.</li><li>Develop vocabulary through description and comparison. For example, it is round like a circle. It is circular.</li><li>Encourage children to make up new lyrics for songs.</li></ul>

How to Use This Book

Use the twenty-six songs on the *Wild, Wild West* CD that is included in this book and the related activities in this book to enhance themes in your curriculum, or use them independently. Either way you have a rich treasure chest of creative ideas for your classroom.

The eight package collection provides more than 200 songs, a perfect combination of the traditional best-loved children's songs and brand new selections created for each theme. Keep a song in your heart and put joy in your teaching!

Bibliography

Bulloch, Kathleen. (2003). *The mystery of modifying: Creative solutions.* Education Service Center, Region VI: Huntsville, Texas.

Cavallaro, Claire & Haney, Michael. (1999). *Preschool inclusion.* Paul H. Brookes Publishing Co: Baltimore, MD.

Gray, Tracy and Fleischman, Steve. "Research matters: Successful strategies for English language learners." *Educational Leadership,* Dec. 2004-Jan. 2005, volume 62, 84-85.

Hanniford, Carla. (1995). *Smart moves: Why learning is not all in your head.* Great Ocean Publications: Arlington, Virginia, p. 146.

LeDoux, Joseph. (1993). "Emotional memory systems in the brain." *Behavioral and Brain Research,* volume 58.

Tabors, Patton O. (1997). *One child, two languages: Children learning English as a second language.* Baltimore, MD: Paul H. Brookes Publishing Co.

Songs and Activities

She'll Be Comin' Round the Mountain

She'll be comin' round the mountain
When she comes.
She'll be comin' round the mountain
When she comes.
She'll be comin' round the mountain,
She'll be comin' round the mountain,
She'll be comin' round the mountain,
When she comes.

She'll be drivin' six white horses
When she comes, (Yee-hah).
She'll be drivin' six white horses
When she comes, (Yee-hah).
She'll be drivin' six white horses,
She'll be drivin' six white horses,
She'll be drivin' six white horses,
When she comes, (Yee-hah).

Oh, we'll all go out to greet her
When she comes, (Howdy).
Oh, we'll all go out to greet her
When she comes, (Howdy).
Oh, we'll all go out to greet her,
Oh, we'll all go out to greet her,
Oh, we'll all go out to greet her,
When she comes, (Howdy).

Oh, we'll all have chicken and
dumplings
When she comes, (Yum, yum).
Oh, we'll all have chicken and
dumplings
When she comes, (Yum, yum).
Oh, we'll all have chicken and
dumplings,
Oh, we'll all have chicken and
dumplings,
Oh, we'll all have chicken and
dumplings
When she comes, (Yum, yum).

She'll be comin' round the mountain
When she comes.
She'll be comin' round the mountain
When she comes.
She'll be comin' round the mountain,
She'll be comin' round the mountain,
She'll be comin' round the mountain,
When she comes.

Vocabulary

chicken and dumplings
driving
greet
horse
mountain
white

Theme Connections

Food and Nutrition
Friends and Families

Did You Know?

○ "She'll Be Comin' Round the Mountain" is a traditional American folk song, written sometime between 1850-1900. No one knows who wrote it.

○ In the Old West, meeting the train or the horse-drawn coach when it came to town was an exciting event. People would meet friends and relatives and get their mail. The song was also used as a work song by people working on the railroad.

○ Animals were used, and still are used, to move people and goods. Humans ride some large animals, use them as pack animals for carrying goods, or harness them, singly or in teams, to pull (or haul) sleds or wheeled vehicles.

Literacy Links

Comprehension

○ Ask the children who they think "she" is? *What does "She'll be driving six white horses" mean?* Ask the children how the song would be different if "she was flying in an airplane" instead of "driving six white horses."

Oral Language

○ Discuss the visit of relatives. *How do your relatives arrive? What do you eat when they come?*

○ Discuss travel in a wagon pulled by horses. *Would the ride be rough or smooth? Would you travel quickly or slowly? What do wagon wheels look like?*

Oral Language/Phonological Awareness

○ Sing the song with the additional verses listed below. Be sure to add the sound effects (echo line) for each verse, for example a whistle sound after red pajamas and a snoring sound after the sleep with grandma line.

> *She'll be wearing red pajamas when she comes…*
> *She will have to sleep with Grandma when she comes…*

Phonological Awareness

○ Discuss *yippee* and *yum-yum*. Challenge the children to think of other words that might be used for the echo on each of these verses in the song. For example, the echo following "she'll be drivin' six white horses" might be "giddy-up." The echo line following "we'll all have chicken and dumplings" might be "um-ummm."

Curriculum Connections

Blocks

○ Help the children place crumpled newspaper under green fabric to create mountains. Have the children build a road around the mountains. Provide plastic horses and a matchbox wagon. Encourage their dramatic play.

○ Suggest that the children use the blocks to fashion a wagon wheel. Provide a model.

Dramatic Play

○ Have the children set the table, cook up some chicken and dumplings, and prepare for the arrival of guests.

Fine Motor

○ Provide clay and have the children shape mountains.

> ✔ **Special Needs Adaptation:** Constructing a mountain from clay with a peer buddy provides the opportunity for a child with disabilities to work collaboratively with others. Even if the child cannot fully participate in the activity, he may be able to participate by helping to move the clay into place or by using a tool such as a kitchen spatula.

Games

○ Teach the children to play Covered Wagon Golf. Cut oatmeal boxes in half. Cover them and print numerals one through eight on them. Place the wagon tops on the floor in a path as you would place croquet hoops. Have the children use a tube to hit a ping-pong ball through the wagon tops in numerical order.

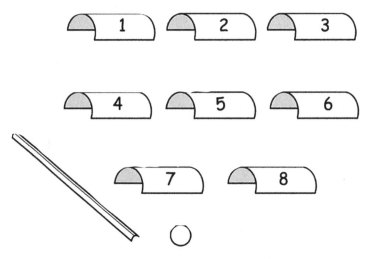

Math

○ A western wagon is typically four feet by ten feet. Give children a sheet of 4" x 10" construction paper (scaled to the size of a wagon bed.) Provide color tiles or a variety of one-inch construction paper squares. Challenge the children to see how many squares it will take to cover the bed of the wagon.

○ Provide small plastic horses in a variety of colors. Ask the children to make sets of six horses. Show them how to create the sets in several different configurations. For example, you might place two horses together and four horses together a few inches away or one horse separated from five horses. Ask questions. *Can you make a set of six white horses? Do you think the horses are harnessed two in a row or three in a row?*

Special Needs Adaptation: For children who are not yet able to work with a set of six horses, use fewer horses. Help the child group her set of horses into various configurations or take four pieces of white paper and write a numeral on each one (1, 2, 3, 4). Invite the child to place the number of horses that corresponds to the number on the paper. For example, if the numeral 2 is written on the paper, she would put two horses on the paper.

Music and Movement

❍ Teach the children "Circle Round the Mountain" to the tune of "Ring Around the Rosie."

Circle Round the Mountain

Circle round the mountain (hold hands and walk around in a circle)
Waiting for the horses
Here they come. Here they come. (stop and shade eyes as if looking left and right)
All jump up. (jump up and down)

Snack

❍ Provide chicken and dumplings for snack. If possible, prepare chicken and dumplings in class. Here is a simple recipe: Pour chicken broth into a crock pot. Add very small pieces of chicken, onion, and celery. Allow the children to tear flour tortillas and put them in the pot. Cook until the chicken is thoroughly cooked. Serve and enjoy!

Writing

❍ Print *yum-yum* on index cards. Ask the children to use magnetic letters to copy the words.

Home Connection

❍ Suggest that children talk about how their relatives arrive when they come to visit.

I'm a Texas Star

I'm a Tex, I'm a Tex,
I'm a Texas star
From way out west
Where the longhorns are.
I can ride 'em, I can rope 'em,
I can show you how it's done.
Come kick up your heels—
It's Texas fun!

Special Needs Adaptation: The vocabulary associated with this song may be difficult for some children. Make picture cards to go with different words, such as longhorn and Texas. Write the name of each word on the card and paste a picture or line drawing above it. Explain each card in detail. Invite the child to help make a sentence using each word. The concept of the direction of west may be too abstract for some children. Label each wall in the classroom with the appropriate direction. Practice using the concept of directions by saying, "Go get the blocks, they are on the west wall" or "Hang up your coat on the rack that is on the east wall."

Vocabulary

kick up your heels
longhorns
ride
rope
star
Texas
west

Theme Connections

Me
Movement

Did You Know?

- Texas is popularly known as the Lone Star State.
- The state's cattle population is estimated to be near 16 million.
- The Texas Rangers, the oldest state law enforcement agency in North America, played an effective, valiant, and honorable role throughout the early troubled years of Texas. The Ranger Service has existed almost continuously from the year of colonization to the present.
- Texas Rangers included Ben McCulloch, the Tennessee frontiersman and friend of Davy Crockett, and William A.A. "Big Foot" Wallace.

Literacy Links

Oral Language

- Discuss cowboys. Make a Word Web. Print *cowboy* in the center of chart paper. Ask the children to tell you what they know about cowboys. Print their information on lines that extend out from the circle.

○ Teach the children the American Sign Language sign for *cowboy* (page 120).

Print Awareness

○ Display a globe or a map. Show the children Texas. Point out the letters in *Texas*. *What letter does* Texas *start with?*

Curriculum Connections

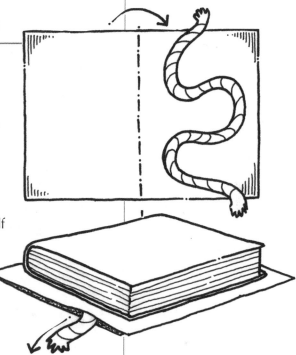

Art

○ Cut easel paper into star shapes. Invite the children to paint the stars.
○ Provide star stencils or templates. Invite the children to make star designs and then color their designs with crayons.
○ Invite the children to make rope designs. Fold a piece of construction paper in half. Dip a piece of rope into tempera paint. Arrange the rope in a design on one half of the construction paper, leaving a small piece of the rope extended past the edge of the paper. Fold the construction paper back in half. Place a book on top of the paper to hold it flat and then pull the end of the rope from between the fold of the paper.

Construction

○ Provide 3" poster board stars and a square of tin foil. Challenge the children to use the foil to wrap the stars.

Discovery

○ Teach the children how to tie a square knot or a slip knot.

Dramatic Play

○ Provide cowboy and cowgirl attire. Encourage the children to explore the western duds. Discuss the purpose of the different western attire. The wide brim of the hat protects the face from the sun. The bandana protects the mouth from dust. The boots protect from stepping on rocks or from being bitten by a snake.

Fine Motor

○ Provide playdough and star cookie cutters. Have the children roll the dough and then cut out star shapes with the cookie cutters.

Book Corner

Cattle Drive! by Jacqueline Ward

Cowboys and Cowgirls: Yippee Yay! by Gail Gibbons

Cowboy Baby by Sue Heap

○ Cut large stars from poster board. Cut the stars into puzzle pieces and invite the children to work the puzzles.

Math

○ Provide pieces of rope cut into 4″, 5″, 6″, 7″, and 8″ sections. Ask the children to arrange the rope pieces from the shortest to the longest. Have them arrange the ropes vertically and horizontally.

Outdoors

○ Ask two volunteers to hold a rope and swing it slowly. Invite the children to jump over the rope while chanting, "I'm a Texas Star."

Social Studies

○ Display a globe. Show the children where the state of Texas is on the globe.

Writing

○ Print *Texas* on drawing paper. Provide small segments of yarn or thin rope and glue. Have the children glue the yarn or rope over the letters.

○ Print *Texas* on index cards. Provide finger paint. Invite the children to use the fingerprint to make fingerprints over the letters in Texas.

Home Connection

○ Suggest that the children ask their families about cowboys.

Skip to My Lou

Vocabulary

buttermilk
cat
darling
fly
partner
shoo
skip
sugar bowl

Theme Connections

Friends and Families
Movement

Lost my partner, what'll I do?
Lost my partner, what'll I do?
Lost my partner, what'll I do?
Skip to my Lou, my darlin'.

Chorus:
Skip, skip, skip to my Lou,
Skip, skip, skip to my Lou,
Skip, skip, skip to my Lou,
Skip to my Lou, my darlin'.

Found me another one, a better one too.
Found me another one, a better one too.
Found me another one, a better one too.
Skip to my Lou, my darlin'.

(Chorus)

Cat's in the buttermilk, what should I do?
Cat's in the buttermilk, what should I do?
Cat's in the buttermilk, what should I do?
Skip to my Lou, my darlin'.

(Chorus)

Fly's in the sugar bowl, shoo, fly, shoo.
Fly's in the sugar bowl, shoo, fly, shoo.
Fly's in the sugar bowl, shoo, fly, shoo.
Skip to my Lou, my darlin'.

(Chorus)

Special Needs Adaptation: Children with special needs, especially those with language delays and/or autism spectrum disorder, have difficulty understanding abstract concepts. Also, when two words sound alike, the child can easily become confused. For example, in this song, *shoo* sounds like the familiar word *shoe*. Even though the meaning is very different, a child with language delays may not understand the way the word *shoo* is used in the song. Explain both meanings to the child. Think of other words that sound alike, such as *bear/bare* and *four/for*. Whenever possible, show pictures or examples that depict each meaning.

Did You Know?

○ "Shoo Fly" was written about Shoo Fly Pies.

○ Shoo Fly Pie is a traditional Pennsylvania Dutch dessert. Brown sugar, molasses, shortening, salt, and spices were all non-perishable ingredients that could survive the long ocean's crossing to America made by German immigrants. The pie's unusual name is said to be due to the fact that pies were traditionally set to cool on windowsills, and because of the sweet ingredients, the cook would constantly have to shoo the flies away.

Literacy Links

Oral Language

○ Discuss the origin of the song. Discuss pies. Which pies are the children's favorites?

Phonological Awareness

○ Print *skip, skip, skip* on chart paper. Ask the children to identify the first letter in each word. Read the three words emphasizing the beginning sounds. Have them read the words with you. Ask a volunteer what sound they hear at the beginning of each word. Point out phrases with a series of words that have the same beginning sound is called *alliteration*.

Curriculum Connections

Art

○ Provide colored chalk and drawing paper. Place a teaspoon of buttermilk on each paper. Show the children how to dip their chalk into the buttermilk for a great new look to the chalk lines.

Games

○ Play partner games.
Back-to-Back Lifts: Children sit back to back with their elbows locked. They try to stand by pushing against each other.
Tug of Peace: Take the Hula Hoops® outdoors and encourage the children to play the Tug of Peace game. It takes cooperative effort. Children sit on either side of the Hula Hoop® and grab hold with both hands. By pulling back on the hoop, they can stand up together.

Gross Motor

○ Place an empty sugar bowl in the middle of the table. Provide plastic flies, or use paper clips to represent flies. Invite the children to attempt to toss flies into the sugar bowl from a distance of at least two feet.

Math

○ Place a 12" line of masking tape on the floor. Have children skip along the line counting the number of skips it takes to reach the end of the line. Next, have them walk the line counting the number of steps it takes to reach the end of the line. Does it take more skips or steps to get to the end of the line?

Music and Movement

○ Teach the children a dance to go with the song.

Shoo fly don't bother me, (walk in a circle to the left)
Shoo fly don't bother me, (walk in a circle to the right)
Shoo fly don't bother me, (walk in a circle to the left)
For I don't want to play. (place hands on hips and shake head no)

Cats in the buttermilk (walk around shooing flies)
Shoo fly, shoo.
Cats in the buttermilk
Shoo fly, shoo.
Cats in the buttermilk
Shoo fly, shoo.
Please just go away. (place hands on hips and shake head no)

Shoo fly don't bother me, (walk to the left in a circle)
Shoo fly don't bother me. (walk to the right in a circle)
Shoo fly don't bother me, (walk to the left in a circle)
Come back another day. (wave good-bye)

Book Corner

Outdoors

○ Teach the children how to skip. Have partners race each other with one child skipping and the other running.

○ Place bulletin board paper on the sidewalk. Provide a tray of tempera paint and flyswatters. Invite the children to dip the flyswatter in the paint and then slap the paint onto the bulletin board paper.

Note: Do this on a warm day when cleanup can be done outdoors with a hose. Be sure the children wear old clothes.

Writing

○ Print *shoo fly* on chart paper. Have the children copy the words with magnetic letters.

Home Connection

○ Encourage the children to check their refrigerators at home for buttermilk. Who has some? Make a chart showing how many children had buttermilk at home.

Dusty by Pam Schiller

Vocabulary

cowboy
horse
name

Theme Connections

Animals
Sounds

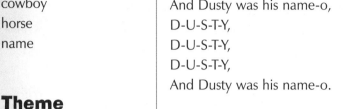

(Tune: Bingo)
There was a cowboy rode a horse,
And Dusty was his name-o,
D-U-S-T-Y,
D-U-S-T-Y,
D-U-S-T-Y,
And Dusty was his name-o.

(Repeat, each time clapping to replace the next letter until the horse's name is clapped entirely.)

Did You Know?

○ A horse's height is measured in hands. One hand equals four inches, which is the width of an average person's hand.

○ Famous cowboys, both real and fictional, often had famous horses. Here are a few of the famous pairs.

Lone Ranger—Silver
Tonto—Scout
Marshall Dillon—Buck
Annie Oakley—Target
Bat Masterson—Stardust
Adam Cartright—Beauty
Little Joe Cartright—Cochise
Zorro—Phantom/Tornado

Literacy Links

Letter Knowledge

○ Print *Dusty* on chart paper. Ask the children to identify each letter. *Which letter is the first letter? Which letter is the last letter?*

Listening

○ Read the listening story, "Quinn and Dusty" (pages 105-106). Have the children call out, "yippee," every time you say Quinn, and call out, "giddy-up," every time you say Dusty.

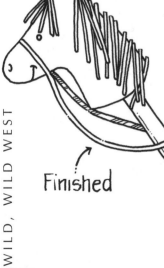

Finished

Oral Language

❍ Teach the children the American Sign Language sign for *cowboy* (page 120).

❍ Use a photograph of a horse to stimulate conversations about horses. Point out the mane, the tail, the nostrils, and the hooves. Tell the children that a horse is measured in hands. Ask a child if you can demonstrate how to measure in hands. Begin at the floor, holding your hand horizontally, fingers together, pinky-side to the floor. Move hand over hand until you reach the top of the head. On a horse, height is measured to the top of the withers, which is the bone at the base of the horse's mane, near the saddle.

✔ **Special Needs Adaptation:** Bring in a toy horse that is large enough for the child to touch. Show the child the eyes and ask him to find the horse's eyes. Then, talk about the horse's legs and count the legs together.

Oral Language/Comprehension

❍ Find pictures to accompany the listening story, "Quinn and Dusty" (page 105). If possible, supply real tools or pictures of real tools used to groom a horse. Explain that *yippee* is a word a cowboy might say when he is happy and *giddy-up* is what a cowboy says to his horse to make it gallop.

Segmentation

❍ Clap the letters in *Dusty*. Challenge the children to think of another name for the cowboy's horse that has five letters. Print the suggested names on chart paper. Clap the letters to make sure there are only five. Sing the song using the new name.

Curriculum Connections

Construction

❍ Construct miniature Stick Horses. Give each child a sturdy straw, a horse head (side view) cut from construction paper, yarn, crayons, tape, and glue. Have the children add the details to their horse heads with crayons and then glue or tape the horse head to their straw. Next, have them cut the yarn into small strips and glue it to the horse's neck for the mane. Cut a longer strip for the bridle.

Dramatic Play

❍ If possible, bring a saddle into the classroom and allow the children to pretend to be riding.

○ Provide Christmas wrapping paper tubes for the children to use as stick horses.

Games

○ Make a Horse Shoe Game. Fill one-half liter soda bottle with sand or pebbles to create a stake. Cut plastic coffee can lids into the shape of horseshoes. Use masking tape to create a throw line. Invite the children to stand behind the throw line and toss the horseshoes onto the stakes.

○ Make two photocopies of the Western Patterns (page 112). Color them, cut them out, and laminate them. Invite the children to play Western Concentration.

> ✓ **Special Needs Adaptation:** Instead of playing a Concentration game, place all the cards face up and ask the child to find the patterns that are alike.

Gross Motor/Outdoor

○ Teach the children how to gallop like a horse.

> ✓ **Special Needs Adaptation:** Horses walk and trot in addition to galloping. For a child with motor challenges, invite him to walk like a horse or trot like a horse.

Language

○ Make a Dusty Name Puzzle. Print *Dusty* on 4" x 12" strips of poster board. Laminate the strips and make puzzle cuts between each letter. Encourage the children to work the Dusty Name Puzzles.

Math

○ Remind the children that horses are measured in hands (each hand is about 4" long). Give the children a 4" piece of yarn and encourage them to find things that are one hand high. Can they find something that is two hands (eight inches) high?

Writing

○ Make a list of famous horse names (see Did You Know? on page 27). Give the children magnetic letters and invite them to copy the names.

Home Connection

○ Suggest that children show their families how to measure the height of their kitchen table in hands.

Cowboy Up by Larry Dane Brimner
I Want to Be a Cowboy by Dan Liebman
My Little Pony: Meet the Ponies by Namrata Trapathi

SONGS AND ACTIVITIES

Move On, Little Dogies

by Pam Schiller

(Tune: My Bonnie Lies Over the Ocean)
The dogies are crossing the prairie.
The dogies are moving along.
The dogies are crossing the prairie,
Come join in our dogie drive song.

Move on, move on, move on little dogies,
Move on, move on.
Move on, move on, move on little dogies,
Move on!

The prairie is grassy and lonely,
The days are long and dry.
At nighttime we'll rest by the campfire
And sleep under the bright starry sky.

Rest now, rest now, rest little dogies,
Rest now, rest now.
Sleep sound, sleep sound,
Tomorrow we'll be homeward bound.

Vocabulary

campfire
crossing
day
dogie
drive
dry
grassy
homeward bound
join
lonely
long
nighttime
prairie
rest
sky
sleep
starry
tomorrow

Theme Connections

Animals
Nighttime

Did You Know?

○ Texas was a perfect location for raising Spanish longhorns and other cattle. The climate was just right, and the land was perfect for grazing. In fact, it was so good that, by the 1800s, there was more beef than the people of Texas knew what to do with. The price of cattle began to drop.

○ Cattle ranchers had to find a new market for their cattle. They knew that people in other parts of the country would buy the cattle, but the problem was how to get the cattle to them. One of the closest rail yards was in Kansas City, Missouri, a long way from Texas.

○ By the 1860s, the price of cattle had dropped so low that ranchers decided it was worthwhile to make the long trip from Texas to Missouri with their cattle. They planned a yearly cattle drive. On a cattle drive, a herd of maybe 2,000 to 3,000 cattle were moved across the open prairie to their destination, grazing as they went. Since the ranchers wanted the cattle to be fattened up when they arrived at the rail yard, the cattle drive moved slowly; the cattle grazed about as much as they walked each day.

○ After dinner, cowboys would sit around the campfire and sing some of their favorite songs. The banjo, fiddle, and harmonica were the most popular trail ride musical instruments. Modern day trail rides still exist and they mimic the rides of the past. Cattle are moved by modern-day cowboys and cowgirls with the same outdoor sleeping arrangements and campfire cooking and music. However, trail rides today are mostly opportunities for participants to re-enact the past. Cattle are no longer driven for long distances as they were in the 1800s. Today, they are shipped by train.

Literacy Links

Comprehension

○ Print *trail rides* in the center of chart paper. Draw a circle around it. Have the children tell you what they know about trail rides. Discuss trail rides. *What do cowboys eat on the trail? Who cooks dinner? How do they write? What do they do at night?* Make a list of things children would like to know about trail rides.

Oral Language

○ Discuss the word *dogies*. Explain that this is a term that cowboys use for motherless calves on the range.

○ Teach the children the American Sign Language sign for *cattle* (page 120).

○ Invite the children to participate in the action story "Going on a Trail Ride" (page 104). Discuss the purpose of trail rides.

Special Needs Adaptation: It will be easier for a child with cognitive challenges to participate in the story if he is already familiar with it. Talk with her about the story and what it means before introducing the story to the entire group. Go over each part and invite the child to join you in acting it out together. Model actions for the child. Then invite her to do it with you.

Curriculum Connections

Dramatic Play

❍ Provide sleeping bags, logs for a pretend fire, metal cooking utensils, and other pretend items for sleeping under the stars. Encourage the children to pretend to be on a trail ride.

Games

❍ Make a large cow head. Add heavy material such as sand or marbles to a plastic milk or juice jug and close securely. Attach the cow's head to the side of the jug. Tie a piece of rope into a lasso. Invite children to try to rope the cow.

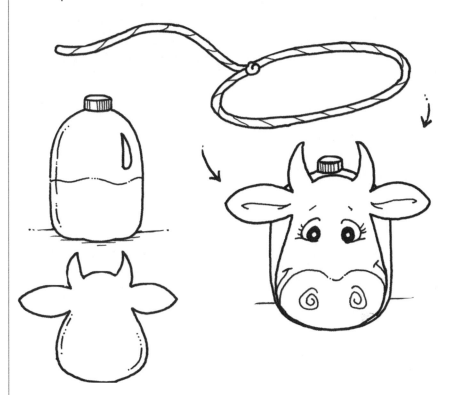

Language

❍ Make and enlarge several photocopies of the cow from the Western Patterns (page 112). Color the cows and laminate them. Cut them into puzzle pieces. Encourage the children to work the puzzle. Talk with the children about how the puzzle pieces fit together.

Math

❍ Tie 16" pieces of rope in circle. Place one numeral card inside each circle. Provide plastic cows and invite the children to count the number of cows into the ropes as indicated by the numeral cards.

Book Corner

The Dirty Cowboy by Amy Timberlake

Sixteen Cows by Lisa Wheeler

Why Cowboys Sleep With Their Boots on by Laurie Lazzaro Knowlton

Music and Movement

○ Make a pretend campfire and sit around it and sing some cowboy songs, for example, "Red River Valley," "You Are My Sunshine" and "Git Along, Little Dogies."

○ Help the children make a kazoo by wrapping wax paper around the teeth of a plastic comb.

Snack

○ Show the children how to make S'mores. Outdoors, build a low fire in an outdoor cooker. Have the children stick a marshmallow on green sticks or opened up coat hangers. Toast the marshmallows over the fire. Show them how to stack one graham cracker, piece of chocolate, their marshmallow and second graham cracker to make a S'more. **Safety Warning:** Supervise and direct the children around the fire and as they roast their marshmallows.

○ Invite the children to follow the Trail Mix Rebus Recipe (page 119) to make their snack. **Allergy Warning:** Check for peanut allergies.

 English Language Learner Strategy: Using a rebus makes it easier for English language learners to follow the directions.

Social Studies

○ Display a map of the USA. Show the children the path that cattle drivers used for their drives in the 1800's. Texas drovers crossed the Red River at Red Rock (near the current town of Preston, Texas), north to Boggy Depot then northeast across the Arkansas River through to Fort Gibson, Baxter Springs, Kansas, and then on to Joplin, Missouri.

Writing

○ Trace around magnetic letters to write *move on* on sheets of drawing paper. Leave a blank space in each word for the letter "o". Provide magnetic letters and encourage the children to fill in the missing letters.

Home Connection

○ Encourage the children to ask their families if they know what cowboys call the cattle they are herding.

Wait for the Wagon

Will you come with me,
    my Phyllis dear,
To yon blue mountain free?
Where the blossoms smell
    the sweetest,
Come rove along with me.

It's every Sunday morning
When I am by your side,
We'll jump into the wagon
And we'll all take a ride.

Chorus:
Wait for the wagon,
Wait for the wagon,
Wait for the wagon,
And we'll all take a ride.

Where the river runs like silver
And the birds they sing so sweet,
I have a cabin, Phyllis,
And something good to eat.

Come listen to my story,
It will relieve my heart;
So jump into the wagon,
And off we will start.

(Chorus)

Together, on life's journey,
We'll travel till we stop,
And if we have no trouble,
We'll reach the happy top.

Then come with me, sweet Phyllis,
My dear, my lovely bride,
We'll jump into the wagon,
And all take a ride.

(Sing the chorus twice.)

Vocabulary

blossom
blue mountain
bride
cabin
happy
journey
morning
ride
river
rove
silver
story
trouble
wagon
yon

Theme Connections

Friends and Families
Transportation

Did You Know?

❍ The words and music of this song were written by R. Bishop Buckley and George P. Knauff. It was first published in Baltimore in 1851. During the Civil War Southerners had a parody, "The Southern Wagon."

The Southern Wagon
Secession is our watchword,
Our rights we will demand;
To defend our homes and firesides
We pledge our hearts and hand.
Jeff Davis is our President,
With Stephen by our side;
Brave Beauregard, our General,
Will join in our ride.

Our wagon is the very best,
The running gear is good;
Stuffed 'round the sides with cotton,
And made of Southern wood.
Carolina is the driver,
With Georgia by her side,
Virginia holds the flag up,
While we all take a ride.

Literacy Links

Oral Language
○ Teach the children the American Sign Language sign for *wagon* (page 121).

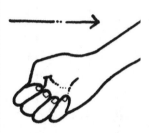

Wagon

Phonological Awareness
○ Challenge the children to think of something that rhymes with *wagon* and that breathes fire. Challenge them to think of something that rhymes with *dragon* that describes the way people describe a wet diaper on a baby. (saggin')

Print Awareness
○ Print *Sunday* on chart paper. Draw a line between *Sun* and *day*. Point out that both *sun* and *day* are words that could stand alone. Explain that when they are put together to make a new word the new word is called a *compound word*.

Curriculum Connections

Art
○ Mix silver glitter or iridescent white glitter in light blue paint. Invite the children to paint rivers that "run like silver."

Blocks
○ Encourage the children to build a wagon or a cabin with the blocks.

Book Corner

Wagon Wheels by
Barbara Brenner
Wagon Train by
Sydelle Kramer
*The Long Way
Westward* by
Joan Sandin

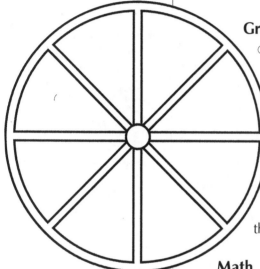

Discovery

❍ Provide cotton balls or powder puffs saturated with floral scents. Make two of each scent. Place the cotton balls or powder puffs inside margarine tubs. Invite the children to lift the lids and smell each scent as they attempt to match the tubs in sets of two.

Dramatic Play

❍ Provide wedding props, such as rings, flowers, clothing and other items. Invite the children to pretend to have a wedding.

Fine Motor

❍ Provide blue playdough. Invite the children to shape "blue mountains."

Gross Motor

❍ Use masking tape to make a wagon wheel with spokes on the floor. Use a piece of tape to make a throw line a short distance from the wagon wheel. Provide a silk flower. Challenge the children to toss the flower between the spokes of the wheel, one section at a time.

Language

❍ Print *Sunday* on an index card and lay it on the table. Give the children a page of a calendar and ask them to circle all the "Sundays" on the page.

Math

❍ Use masking tape to section an area on the floor that is 4' x 10', the size of a pioneer wagon. Have the children sit inside the sectioned off spot on the floor to determine how many children could fit inside a covered wagon.

Outdoors

❍ Turn a wagon upside down and encourage the children to examine the wagon's wheels.

Home Connection

❍ Suggest that the children ask their family members what they like most about being a family.

The Rodeo by Pam Schiller

Vocabulary

boots
bucking bulls
calves
clown
cotton candy
cowboy
dandy
hat
popcorn
rodeo

Theme Connections

Animals
Clowns

(Tune: Row, Row, Row Your Boat)
Hats, boots, and funny clowns
People all around.
Popcorn, drinks and cotton candy
Cowboys looking dandy.

Yippee, yipeee yo, kiya
Yippee, yo, kiya
Yippee, yipeee yo, kiya
Yippee, yo, kiya!

Restless calves and bucking bulls
Children from local schools
The rodeo starts today
Yippee, yo, kiya!

Yippee, yipeee yo, kiya
Yippee, yo, kiya
Yippee, yipeee yo, kiya
Yippee, yo, kiya!

Did You Know?

- Rodeo clowns put themselves in danger every time they go to work. With names like Shane, Flint, Cody, Scooter, and Tex, they evoke the nostalgia of the old west. They wear painted-on smiles and baggy britches. And they actually like it when people laugh at them, even as they risk their lives to protect others.

- It may look like fun and games to the people in the stands, but this is serious business, and not just any clown can do it. Between rides, the barrel man's job is to keep the crowd amused by bantering with the announcers and performing comedic skits that can include props, explosions, fireworks, clown cars, and sometimes lucky members of the audience. This part requires charisma, creativity, comic timing, and boundless energy.

- The real work—cowboy protection—begins the minute a bull rider enters the ring, hanging on for dear life. And this part requires nerves of steel, lightning reflexes, and a selfless devotion to someone else's well-being. It falls to the rodeo clown to distract the angry bull from its toppled rider so the cowboy can get to his feet and make it to the safety of a fence.

○ Nowadays rodeo clowns have a little more technology in their corner, by way of an invention some years back by a bullfighter named Jasbo. The "clown lounge," as some call it, is made of heavy-gauge steel, weighs 175 pounds, and is lined with industrial foam rubber. But just because a barrel protects the man inside doesn't mean it's invincible—not with 3,000- to 4,000-pound horned bulls on attack.

○ See page 90 for more information about rodeos.

Literacy Links

Oral Language

○ Print *Rodeo* on chart paper. Draw a circle around the word. Discuss rodeos. Have the children tell you everything they know about rodeos. Write their information on lines that extend from the circled word.

Phonological Awareness

○ Challenge the children to brainstorm a list of words that rhyme with clown, such as *down, drown, frown, town* and so on.

Phonological Awareness/Print Awareness

○ Print *kiya* on chart paper. Replace the first letter with other letters, such as tiya, hiya, miya, biya, and so on. Sing the song using replacement words for kiya. *Do you like any of the other words better?*

Curriculum Connections

Art

○ Provide pale pink paint and encourage the children to paint cotton candy.

Blocks

○ Provide plastic rodeo animals. Encourage the children to build a rodeo arena with fenced pens for all the rodeo animals.

Dramatic Play

○ Provide clown costumes and western wear. Invite the children to dress like rodeo clowns and dandy cowpokes.

Games

❍ Make two copies of the Western Patterns (page 112). Color them, cut them out, and laminate them. Encourage the children to use the cards to play western concentration.

Gross Motor

❍ Start a stopwatch while the children jump up and down. Let individual children see how long they can jump. Point out that the stopwatch is used when a cowboy is riding a bull. It tells everyone how long the cowboy stayed on the bull.

Language

❍ Provide photos of rodeo animals, bulls, calves, dogs, pigs, goats, and horses. Encourage the children to pick the animal that they like best.

Special Needs Adaptations: Ask the child to name the animal in each picture. If he does not know the animal's name, tell him. For example, say, "This is a horse," and point to the picture of the horse. After the child learns the name of each animal, invite him to make sentences with each picture. If the child is unable to make a sentence, model one for him by using a technique called *slotting*. This strategy is similar to fill-in-the-blank except that the word the child needs to add is provided for him. For example, say, "A pig has a tail that is curly." Ask the child to point to the pig's tail, and then say, "The pig has a _____ tail." Even if the child does not say *curly*, it is okay, as along as the word that is provided by the child will fit. For example, the child may say "short" or "little." While that is not the specific word you are looking for, it is a word that will work in the sentence. If the child answers with a word that will not fit, such as, "The pig has a (cup) tail," do not tell the child he is wrong. Instead, say, "Let's look at the pig's tail together. It is curly and it is short." Repeat this activity with all the animal picture cards.

Snack

❍ Provide popcorn for snack. Provide a variety of seasonings for the popcorn, such as cinnamon and sugar, parmesan cheese, and seasoned salt for the children to sample.

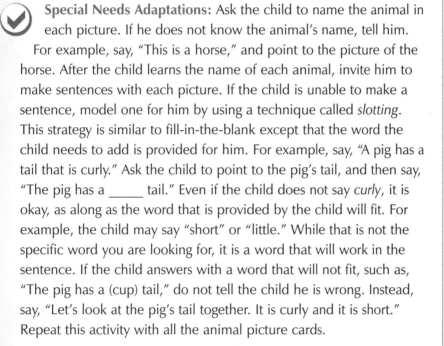

Book Corner

Armadillo Rodeo by
Jan Brett
*Bill Pickett: Rodeo-
Ridin Cowboy* by
Andrea Davis
Pickney
*Lasso Lou and
Cowboy McCoy*
by Barbara
Larmon Failing

Special Event

○ Have your own rodeo. Invite the children to wear their western duds. Invite families to participate. Play games like Horseshoes and Pin the Tail on the Bull. Serve Cowboy Stew (page 106) or Beans and Wienies and Buckaroo Cookies (page 113)

○ Take photos of the children doing all the steps in making Buckaroo Cookies. Make copies of the photos and encourage the children to sequence them. You can also display the photos during your rodeo.

Writing

○ Trace magnetic letters to write "yippee, yo, kiya" on index cards or drawing paper. Provide magnetic letters and encourage the children to lay the letters over the correct letters on the index cards or drawing paper.

Home Connection

○ Invite families to help plan and attend a rodeo day.

Home on the Range

Vocabulary

amazed
antelope
bright
browse
cloudy
deer
discouraging
eagle
flower
frontier
gazed
glory
home
light
night
prairie
range
roam
rock
scream
seldom
shrill
sky
star

Theme Connections

Animals
Friends and Families
Homes

Oh, give me a home
Where the buffalo roam,
And the deer and the antelope
    play.
Where seldom is heard
A discouraging word,
And the sky is not cloudy all day.

Chorus:
Home, home on the range!
Where the deer and the antelope
    play.
Where seldom is heard
A discouraging word,
And the sky is not cloudy all day.

I love the bright flowers
In this frontier of ours,
And I thrill to the eagle's shrill
    scream.
Blood red are the rocks,
Brown the antelope flocks
That browse on the prairie so
    green.

(Chorus)

How often at night
When the heavens are bright
With the light of the unclouded
    stars,
Have I stood here amazed
And asked as I gazed,
If their glory exceeds that of ours.

(Chorus)

Where seldom is heard
A discouraging word,
And the sky is not cloudy all day.

Did You Know?

○ The words to "Home on the Range" are from a poem by Dr. Brewster M. Higley. Higley was an early pioneer of Smith County, Kansas in 1871. The poem was called "Oh Give Me a Home." Dan Kelley wrote the music. The Harlan Brother orchestra was the first to play the song. It was recorded in April 1873 at a dance that was held at the Harlan home. It was a hit from the start and it spread over the country as if by magic. The song was picked up by settlers, cowboys, and others and spread across the nation in various forms.

○ The words were altered slightly from the original poem that began "A home, a home where the deer and the antelope play. The first line was changed to "Home, home on the range, where the deer and the antelope play," as it is sung today.

○ This song was officially adopted by the state of Kansas as its state song on June 30, 1947.

Literacy Links

Comprehension/Oral Language
○ Discuss houses and home. *What makes a house a home?*

Oral Language
○ Have the children say *range*. Have the children use *range* in a sentence.
○ Teach the children the American Sign Language sign for *home* (page 120).

Print Awareness
○ Print *Home, Sweet, Home* on chart paper. Have the children copy the words on drawing paper to make a special sign for their home. Provide crayons and paints and invite children to decorate their signs.

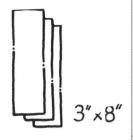

3" x 8"

Curriculum Connections

Art
○ Provide large colorful silk or plastic flowers and invite the children to make floral arrangements for their prairie home.
○ Provide small white stars for children to glue on a large sheet of black bulletin board paper or on individual sheets of black construction paper.

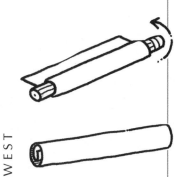

Blocks
○ Provide log-type blocks and invite the children to build a range home, Provide cattle, antelope, deer, and horses to graze in on the prairie grass.

Construction
○ Cut 3" x 8" strips from grocery sacks. Show the children how to roll the paper around a pencil to make logs. Remove the pencil and use tape to keep the paper roll together. Challenge them to glue the logs together to build a prairie house.

Dramatic Play
○ Suggest the children set up a "range" home. Don't forget to add a "Home, Sweet Home" sign.

Language
○ Take photographs of the children making their prairie houses (see the Construction activity). Challenge the children to arrange the photos in the sequence of the building of a prairie house.
○ Have the children dictate a sentence about their home. Have them illustrate their sentence.

> ✓ **Special Needs Adaptation:** If a child is unable to dictate a sentence about her home, help her by asking questions. Ask the child's family to send a picture of her home to school. Encourage the child to draw a picture of her home.

Math
○ Collect five berry baskets to represent five corrals, or build five corrals with blocks. Print numerals 1-5 on index cards and place one card in each corral. Provide plastic cows. Encourage the children to count the correct number of cows into the corrals.

Outdoors
○ Take the children outdoors to observe the clouds. *Is it a cloudless day?*

Home Connection

○ Have the children make "Home, Sweet Home" signs for their homes.

Billy Boy

Oh, where have you been, Billy Boy, Billy Boy?
Oh, where have you been charming Billy?
I've been to seek a wife, she's the joy of my life,
She's a young thing, and cannot leave her mother.

Did she ask you to come in, Billy Boy, Billy Boy?
Did she ask you to come in charming Billy?
Yes, she asked me to come in, with a dimple in her chin,
She's a young thing and cannot leave her mother.

Did she set for you a chair, Billy Boy, Billy Boy?
Did she set for you a chair charming Billy?
Yes, she set for me a chair, she has ringlets in her hair,
She's a young thing and cannot leave her mother.

Can she bake a cherry pie, Billy Boy, Billy Boy?
Can she bake a cherry pie, charming Billy?
She can bake a cherry pie fast as a cat can wink her eye,
She's a young thing and cannot leave her mother.
She's a young thing and cannot leave her mother.

Vocabulary

cat
chair
charming
cherry pie
chin
dimple
eye
joy
ringlets
wink
young

Theme Connections

Food and Nutrition
Friends and Families
Humor

Did You Know?

○ "Billy Boy" has been a favorite square dance tune and fiddle tune since the 1800s. Some people think that it is a takeoff on an old English song called, "Lord Randall." Lord Randall is a tense dialogue between Lord Randall and his mother, during which dawns the awful realization that he has been poisoned by his lover and is going to die. A more modern version of "Billy Boy" was recorded in 1965 as "My Boy, Willie" by Burl Ives.

Literacy Links

Comprehension

○ Make up hand motions to accompany the song. For example, roll pie dough while singing "can she bake a cherry pie," and point to a chair while singing "did she offer you a chair."

Letter Knowledge/Phonological Awareness

❍ Print *Billy Boy* on chart paper. Have the children identify the first letter in each word. Tell the children that when two or more words with the same first letter are placed together in a phrase or a sentence they create a sound that is called alliteration. Encourage the children make up an alliterative name for each classmate. For example, Cheerful Charlie.

Oral Language

❍ Discuss color words that can be used to describe the words used in the song. For example, red to describe the cherry pie.

✔ **Special Needs Adaptation:** Make a set of color cards. Take plain white index cards and glue a different color cloth or colored paper square on each card. Hold up the card and ask the child to find something that matches the color on the card. If necessary, model for the child what you want him to do. For example, hold up the card with the red square on it and say, "I am looking for something that is this color." (If the child is nonverbal or has not yet learned the color names, continue by saying, "This square is red" and then point to an object that is that color. "Look, _____ (use the child's name) I see a shirt that is red." Direct the child toward where you are looking and say, "See? Marcus is wearing a red shirt." Then say to the child, "Do you see something that is red?" or "Point to something that is red." If this is too overwhelming for the child, select some simple classroom objects, such as blocks, counters, or toys in a variety of colors. Place three on the table and say, "Point to the toy (block, counter, and so on) that is red." Then, hold up the red card. Some children with disabilities have trouble with too many choices. Especially when a child is just learning to identify colors, it may be easier for him to select an item from a group of two or three. It is, however, very important that you reinforce the concept you are teaching and that you vary the items. Allow the child to practice with one color before moving to another color. Also, practice the colors he knows, before adding new ones.

Oral Language/Comprehension

❍ Point out the question-and-answer format of the song. Print the song on chart paper. Point out the question marks.

Phonological Awareness

❍ Discuss the rhyming word pairs in the song, *wife/life in/chin,* and *pie/eye.* Challenge children to write a new verse to the song. (Can she dance an Irish jig, Can she sing a silly song, and so on)

Book Corner

B Is for Buckaroo by
Louise Doak
Whitney and
Gleaves Whitney
Cowboys by Teri
Martin
*If You'll Be My
Valentine* by
Cynthia Rylant

Curriculum Connections

Discovery
○ Show the children how to use a plastic knife to curl paper ribbons into ringlets.

Dramatic Play/Fine Motor
○ Provide small pie tins, rolling pins, uncolored playdough, and red playdough. Show the children how to roll the uncolored playdough for a pie crust and how to roll the red playdough into small ball for cherries for the pie.
○ Provide mirrors and encourage the children to practice winking.

Fine Motor
○ Provide playdough, yarn, and wiggle eyes. Encourage the children to make a face. Show them how to use their fingers to make a dimple in the chin.

Games
○ Play Cooperative Musical Chairs. Divide the class into two groups. Place two less chairs than children with each group. Play music and have the children circle the chairs. When the music stops children need to find a chair to sit on even if it is a chair they are sharing with a friend. Continue until there is only one chair in each group. Help children find a way that they can share the space on the single chair. Everyone wins!

Language
○ Use six-inch paper plates, yarn, construction paper, markers, wiggle eyes, and other art supplies to make two or three Billy Boy Puppets and two or three fiancées. Glue the faces to tongue depressors to create puppets. Invite the children to use the puppets for dramatic play.

Snack
○ Provide small pre-cooked pie shells and cherry pie filling. Allow the children to scoop pie filling into a shell and then eat it.

Writing
○ Print *Billy Boy* on index cards. Provide red tempera paint to represent cherry juice. Have the children cover the letters with "cherry" fingerprints.

Home Connection

○ Encourage children to ask their moms and dads what kind of pie they like.

The Yellow Rose of Texas

Vocabulary

banjo
belles
break my heart
bright
dew
diamonds
fellow
forevermore
rose
sparkle
woe
yellow
yore

Theme Connections

Colors
Friends and Families
Music

There's a yellow rose of Texas
That I am going to see,
No other fellow knows her,
No other, only me.
She cried so when I left her,
It like to break my heart,
And if I ever find her
We never more will part.

She's the sweetest rose of color
A fellow ever knew,
Her eyes are bright as diamonds,
They sparkle like the dew.
You may talk about your dearest
   May
And sing of Rosa Lee,
But the Yellow Rose of Texas
Beats the belles of Tennessee.

Oh, now I'm going to find her,
For my heart is full of woe,
And we'll sing the song together,
That we sang long ago;
We'll play the banjo gaily,
And we'll sing the songs of yore,
And the Yellow Rose of Texas
Shall be mine forevermore.
And the Yellow Rose of Texas
Shall be mine forevermore.

Did You Know?

❏ The original song title was "Emily, the Maid of Morgan's Point." The song was inspired by the heroic acts of Emily D. West, a slave who James Morgan purchased in New York and then converted to a 99-year indentured servant.

❏ In 1836, during the end of the war with Mexico for Texas' independence, Emily West was working on land owned by James Morgan near the San Jacinto Bay, where the last great battle of the war for the independence of Texas was fought. Because of Emily's bravery during this last battle, James Morgan repealed her indentured status and gave her passage back to New York. Morgan made certain everyone knew of Emily's heroism.

❏ Today, the heroic acts of the young slave woman from New York are still respectfully commemorated by the members of the Knights of the Yellow Rose of Texas each spring at San Jacinto.

Literacy Links

Oral Language

○ Teach the children the American Sign Language sign for *I love you* (page 121).

Oral Language/Comprehension

○ Ask children how the song would be different if it were about a red, red rose instead of a yellow rose.

> **Special Needs Adaptation:** Focus on teaching children about roses. Bring in a live rose (or, if possible, one for each child). Create a small learning circle by inviting children with special needs and those who are English language learners to join the group and explore the qualities of roses. Hold up a rose and show the children how to hold it without being stuck by the thorns. Next, pass the rose around (if some children are afraid because of the thorns, you can hold it for them). Allow each child to smell the rose's fragrance. Talk about rose petals. Put the rose in water and place it in the classroom for all the children to enjoy.

Phonological Awareness

○ Challenge children to think of words that rhyme with *rose*.

Curriculum Connections

Art

○ Provide crayons, glue, glitter, or rhinestones. Encourage the children to draw a picture of "The Yellow Rose of Texas." Suggest that children use the rhinestones or glitter for her eyes. Remind them that she had eyes that sparkle like diamonds.
○ Provide yellow paint and encourage the children to paint roses.

Fine Motor

○ Provide flower catalogs, scissors, and glue. Encourage the children to create a flower collage.

Language

○ Provide the Rose Rhyming Word Cards (page 109). Encourage the children to select the pictures that rhyme with rose.

Book Corner

Music

❍ Provide a banjo to explore or provide banjo music to listen to.

Science

❍ Use floral scents to scent cotton balls or powder puffs. Make one of each scent except for rose. Make two rose scents. Place the scented cotton balls or powder puffs in margarine tubs. Have the children smell the rose scent and then smell each of the other scents to identify the matching scent.

Social Studies

❍ Show the children where Texas is on a globe or a map. Show them the Houston area. Explain that the woman who inspired the song lived in this area. Show the children where Tennessee is on the globe.

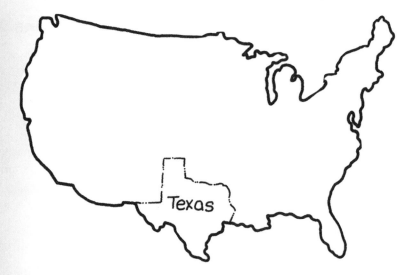

Writing

❍ Print *rose* on index cards. Provide yellow markers and tracing paper and invite the children to trace over the letters.

Home Connection

❍ Suggest that children show their families the yellow rose they painted and tell their families about the song.

Trigger

(Tune: Five Little Ducks)
My little horsie's name is Trigger
He ate so much he got bigger and bigger.
His mouth chomp-chomps and his tail goes swish.
And when he trots, he clip-clap clomps!
Chomp, chomp,
Swish, clip,
Clap, clomp!

Vocabulary

bigger
chomp
clap
clomp
swish
tail
trot

Theme Connections

Animals
Sounds

Did You Know?

❍ Horses belong to the *equus* family. *Equus* comes from the ancient Greek word meaning quickness.

❍ Horses are mammals in the same family as zebras, mules, and donkeys.

❍ A stallion is a male horse, and a mare a female horse.

❍ Baby horses are called foals, males are colts and females are fillies. Young horses are called colts and fillies up until the age of three. When foals are a year old they are called yearlings.

❍ A pony is not a baby horse. It is a fully-grown small horse.

❍ Horses love to eat short, juicy grass. They also eat hay (which is dried grass) especially in the winter or when they are stabled. High-energy foods, such as barley, oats, maize, chaff, bran, or processed pony nuts, are good for working horses. Horses have small stomachs for their size and need to eat little and often. When in a field, horses will graze for most of the day.

❍ A horse's tail is very important. Not only does it act as a flyswatter in summer, it keeps his "bottom" warm in winter!

Literacy Links

Comprehension

❍ Display a photograph of a horse. Prepare a KWL chart as follows. Make a three-column chart on chart paper. Label the first column "What We Know."

Ask children to tell you what they know about horses and note their comments in the first column. Label the second column "What We Would Like to Know." Ask the children what they would like to know and list that information in the second column. Label the third column "What We Have Learned" and fill it in at the end of each day or at the end of study.

Listening
○ Read the story, "Quinn and Dusty" (page 105). Change the horse's name from Dusty to Trigger. Have the children call out, "Yippee!" every time you say, "Quinn," and call out, "Giddy-up," every time you say, "Trigger."

Oral Language
○ Teach the children the American Sign Language sign for *horse* (page 121).

Phonological Awareness
○ Discuss the *onomatopoeic* words (words that imitate the sound they are describing) in the song—clip-clap, clomp, swish, clip, and clap.

Segmentation
○ Clap the syllables in the word *Trigger*. Have the children think of other names for horses that are two syllables.

Curriculum Connections

Construction
○ Help the children make a pretend horse's tail. Provide strips of paper, ribbon, or newspaper. Suggest that children gather several strands and then use masking tape to wrap the strands together. Have the children swish the pretend tails to see if they can create a swishing sound.

Discovery
○ Display different types of horse foods, such as barley, oats, and maize (corn). Have the children examine the foods. *Are they hard or soft? What kind of noise would a horse making chewing each type of food?*

Book Corner

Fine Motor/Games

❍ Make a Feed the Horse Game. Photocopy the horse from the Western Patterns (page 112). Color it, cut it out, and glue it to the side of a box. Use a mat knife to cut a hole close to the horse's mouth. Provide tweezers and corn. Encourage the children to pick up the corn with the tweezers and drop it into the hole in the box to feed the horse.

Games

❍ Make two photocopies of the Western Patterns (page 112). Color them, cut them out, and laminate them. Give them to the children and encourage them to play Western Concentration.

Sand and Water Play

❍ Place hay in the sand and water table. Hide washers or buttons in the hay. Have the children search for lost items in the hay. Ask questions. *How does hay feel? Is it sticky?*

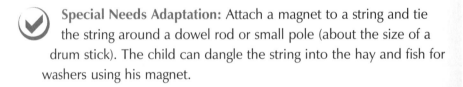
Special Needs Adaptation: Attach a magnet to a string and tie the string around a dowel rod or small pole (about the size of a drum stick). The child can dangle the string into the hay and fish for washers using his magnet.

Snack

❍ Invite the children to use the Haystack Rebus Recipe (page 114) to make snack. **Allergy Warning:** Check for peanut allergies.

Writing

❍ Trace magnetic letters on strips of poster board to form *Trigger*. Leave enough space between each letter to cut the letters apart using a puzzle cut. Color the letters and cut them apart. Invite the children to work the puzzles.

Home Connection

❍ Suggest children teach their families the American Sign Language sign for *horse*.

Buffalo Gals

Vocabulary

buffalo
dance
foot
gals
heel
knockin'
light
meet
moon
pretty
sidewalk
silvery
stockin'
street
toe
tonight

Theme Connections

Friends and Families
Movement
Music
Nighttime

Chorus:
Buffalo gals, won't you come out tonight,
Come out tonight, come out tonight?
Buffalo gals, won't you come out tonight
And dance by the light of the moon?

As I was walking down the street,
Down the street, down the street,
A pretty little gal I chanced to meet,
Under the silvery moon.

(Chorus)

I stopped her and we had a talk,
Had a talk, had a talk.
Her feet took up the whole sidewalk
And left no room for me.

(Chorus)

I asked her if she'd have a dance,

Have a dance, have a dance.
I thought that I might have a chance
To shake a foot with her.

(Chorus)

I danced with a gal with a hole in her stockin',
And her heel kept a-knockin', and her toes kept a-rockin'.
I danced with a gal with a hole in her stockin'
As we danced by the light of the moon.

(Chorus)

And dance by the light of the moon.
And dance by the light of the moon.

Did You Know?

- ○ Millions of Americans have ancestors who immigrated to the United States from Europe and took the Erie Canal to get to the Great Lakes and settle in the Midwest. The mighty city of Chicago, for example, was a direct beneficiary of population brought by the canal. The canal began in Albany and ended in Buffalo, NY, and was built with a large amount of immigrant labor.
- ○ "Buffalo Gals Won't You Come Out Tonight," was written about women in Buffalo during this time in history.

Literacy Links

Oral Language

❍ Discuss some of the unusual phases in the song like "shake a foot with her" and "her feet took up the whole sidewalk."

❍ Teach children the American Sign Language sign for *moon* (page 121) and *girl* (page 120).

Print Awareness

❍ Print the chorus on chart paper. Move your hand under the words as the children sing the chorus. Point out the left-to-right and top-to-bottom direction of the words. Point out the question marks.

Special Needs Adaptation: Give each child a card with a large question mark (?) on it. Encourage them to hold up their card with a question mark on it when they want to ask a question. If the child is unable to ask a question, model one for him. Continue, until everyone has a chance to both ask and answer a question. Reinforce the activity by asking questions throughout the day.

Curriculum Connections

Construction

❍ Invite the children to make Buffalo Gal Puppets. Provide two 6" paper plates, four 12" strips of construction paper, yarn, a cut-out cowboy hat, crayons, and glue for each child. Show children how to glue the plates together to create a body and a head. Then have them fan-fold the strips of construction paper for the arms and legs and glue them in place. Next have the children use the crayons and markers to create facial features. Cut the yarn into strips and glue it on for hair and then add the cowboy hat. Show the children how to make their puppets dance.

Discovery

❍ Place a light source in an area close to an empty wall space. Encourage the children to dance between the light source and the wall to create shadow dancers on the wall. Tell the children that the light source is the moon and that they are creating moon shadows as they "dance by the light of the moon."

Dramatic Play

❍ Provide different types of stockings for children to explore.

Gross Motor

○ Bring the large foot used in the Outdoors activity (below) indoors and tape it to the floor. Invite the children to try to jump over the foot.

Music and Movement

○ Teach the children a dance to accompany the song. Have them join hands to make a circle. Follow the directions with the song.

Outdoors

○ Have the children see how many heel-to-toe steps it takes to walk across the sidewalk. Cut a large foot from bulletin board paper to span the distance across the sidewalk. Remind the children that the words in the song say that the pretty girl's feet "took up the whole sidewalk and left no room for me."

Social Studies

○ Use a map to show the children the Erie Canal. Point out the town of Buffalo, NY.

Writing

○ Print *buffalo* on chart paper. Encourage the children to copy it with markers or with magnetic or felt letters.

Home Connection

○ Encourage the children to sing the chorus of the song to their families. Does anyone at home know this song? The next day, ask the children if their family members knew this song.

SONGS AND ACTIVITIES

Tiny Cowboy Joe

by Pam Schiller and Richele Bartkowiak

(Tune: Turkey in the Straw)
I know a tiny cowboy from way out west.
He wears red boots and a yellow cowboy vest.
He rides a jackalope and his name is Joe,
And he plays a dancin' tune on his old banjo.

Chorus:
Dance to the music—kick up your heels.
Spin on your toes just see how it feels.
Swing your partner, do-si-do,
No one plays better music than tiny cowboy Joe.

Joe's jackalope is rootin'-tootin' dandy
Hanging from his antlers are toys and candy
His ears are droopy and his feet are long
And he spins on his tail when Joe plays this song.

(Chorus)

When the sun begins to set, Joe gives a little sigh.
He jumps on his jackalope and waves goodbye.
As he rides down the trail—dusty and long,
You can hear little Joe whistling this song.

(Chorus)

Vocabulary

antlers	partner
banjo	rootin'
cowboy	sigh
dandy	sigh
do-si-do	spins
droopy	swing
dusty	tiny
floppy	tootin'
good-bye	trail
heel	vest
jackalope	west
music	whistle

Theme Connections

Animals
Movement
Music
Sounds

Did You Know?

❍ Whiplash, a rough-ridin' cowboy monkey from Texas, is a featured star in Dodge World's Toughest Rodeo. He is billed as "the world's smallest cowboy."

❍ Whiplash weighs just seven pounds, but when it comes to staying in the saddle on a big, bucking border collie and herding a few sheep, he hangs (on) tough. Whiplash's two latest mounts are Ben and Bud. They alternate performances. Whiplash doesn't care which one he rides.

○ The jackalope is a mythical combination of a jackrabbit and an antelope (or sometimes a goat or deer), and it is usually portrayed as a rabbit with antlers. It is also called an antelabbit or stagbunny.

Literacy Links

Oral Language

○ Discuss the humor in the song. *What would a small cowboy look like riding on a jack rabbit? How small would the cowboy have to be?*

○ Teach the children the American Sign Language sign for *cowboy, hat,* and *boots* (page 120).

○ Show the children a picture of a cowboy and/or a saddle. Discuss the parts of a cowboy's outfit (bandana, belt, hat, chaps, spurs) or a saddle (horn, stirrups, seat, pommel). Encourage the children to use *cowboy* and *saddle* in a sentence.

 Special Needs Adaptation: If a child can't use *cowboy* or *saddle* in a sentence, make a sentence for him and ask him to fill in the blanks.

Curriculum Connections

Art

○ Provide crayons and paper. Encourage the children to draw Joe.

Construction

○ Help the children make Western hats. Take five sheets of newspaper and stack them unevenly. Place the newspaper on a child's head. Wrap masking tape around the crown of his head to create the bowl of the hat. Take the hat off the child's head and help him roll the edges of the paper to make the brim. Invite the children to paint their hats. Provide a star template for them to trace if they want to add stars to their hats. Provide ribbon and feathers for the hatband.

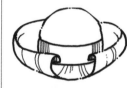

○ Help the children make a Tiny Joe Vest. Cut armholes and a neck from a large grocery sack. Slit the sack up the middle on one side. Fringe the open end of the sack. Provide yellow paint and an assortment of decorative items such a stars, buttons, and rickrack for the children to use to decorate their vests.

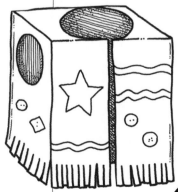

Discovery

○ Make homemade banjos. Place thin and wide rubber bands around different sizes of cake pans. Invite the children to explore the banjo sounds they can make by strumming the rubber bands. **Safety Note:** Supervise closely and make sure that children understand that if they stretch and then release a rubber band it can break and hurt them.

Fine Motor

○ Use small branches from a tree to replicate antlers. Follow the directions under Games (below) to make hanging cards from the Western Patterns (page 112). Give the children straws and challenge them to hang a Western picture on the end of their straw and then onto an antler.

Games

○ Play Drop the Bandana as you would play Drop the Handkerchief.

○ Play Are You the Cowboy? Make photocopies of the Western Patterns (page 112). Make enough copies so that each child will have one of the Western pictures. Select one child to be IT. Have IT stand in the middle of the circle and ask children, one at a time, "Are you the cowboy?" The children answer according to the picture in their hands. If the selected child is not holding the cowboy picture, he answers according to the picture he is holding, for example, "No, I am the horse." When IT finally finds the cowboy, she goes to the circle, receives a card, and sits down. The child who was the cowboy becomes the new IT.

○ Use small branches to replicate a pair of antlers. Photocopy the Western Patterns (page 112). Color the patterns, if desired, and then cut them out and laminate them. Punch a small hole in the top of each picture and string a six-inch piece of yarn through the hole so the pictures can be hung on the "antlers." Give the children clues and have them locate the picture on the antlers that corresponds to your clue. For example, you may say, "find the item that cowboy Joe wears on his head" or "find the item that a cowboy uses for transportation."

Music and Movement

○ Invite the children to dance freely to the song. Encourage them to follow the directions in the chorus.

 Special Needs Adaptation: Ask the child to wave a scarf in time to the music. Or, in keeping with the theme of the song, wave a bandana.

Oh, Susanna

Vocabulary

Alabama
banjo
buckwheat cake
dream
hot
knee
Louisiana
mouth
night
South
still
tear
weather

Theme Connections

Friends and Families
Nighttime
Weather

I come from Alabama
With my banjo on my knee.
I'm going to Louisiana,
My true love for to see.

It rained all night the day I left.
The weather it was dry.
The sun so hot, I froze to death,
Susanna, don't you cry.

Chorus:
Oh, Susanna,
Oh don't you cry for me,
For I come from Alabama
With my banjo on my knee.

I had a dream the other night
When everything was still.
I thought I saw Susanna
A-coming down the hill.

The buckwheat cake was in her mouth.
The tear was in her eye.
Says I, "I'm coming from the South,
Susanna, don't you cry."

(Chorus)

Special Needs Adaptation: Discuss the opposite pairs—wet and dry and hot and cold—in the song. Some children with special needs, especially those with cognitive challenges, often learn best when they experience what you are trying to teach them. Hold up a wet paper towel and say, "This is wet." Pass the towel around for everyone to feel. Next, hold up a dry paper towel. Say, "This is dry" and pass it around. Repeat, with other examples, and then do the same thing with the concept of hot/cold. Reinforce these two sets of opposites, before trying to add new ones. After you have practiced with these opposites, add others, such as in/out, on/off, and up/down. Remember to reinforce and practice each one, using real-life examples.

Did You Know?

○ "Oh, Susanna" was written by Stephen Foster in 1854. Foster was born on July 4, 1826 in Pennsylvania. Many historians agree that "Oh, Susanna" was the first popular song that everyone can still recognize and sing today that was written by an American.

Literacy Links

Comprehension

○ Discuss the contradictions in the verse that says "it rained all night the day I left, the weather it was dry" and "the sun so hot, I froze to death." *Can both things in the sentences be true?* Discuss the opposite pairs: wet/dry and hot/cold.

Letter Knowledge

○ Print *Susanna* on chart paper. Ask the children to identify the letters. Ask questions. *Which letters appear in the name twice? Are any of the letters made using straight lines?*

Print Awareness

○ Show the children a globe or a map. Point out all the locations mentioned in the song—Alabama, Louisiana, and the Southern part of the United States. Show them that each state is labeled.

Segmentation

○ Snap the syllables in *Susanna*. Find children who have a name that is three syllables, and snap the syllables in their names.

Curriculum Connections

Discovery

○ Make a banjo by stretching rubber bands over a shallow cake pan. Use different widths and lengths of rubber bands. Challenge children to listen for the differences in sounds between small and large rubber bands. Challenge them to listen for differences in sounds between wide and narrow rubber bands. **Safety Warning:** Warn the children about the danger of stretching rubber bands and letting them go.

Listening

○ Provide banjo music CDs and invite the children to enjoy the music. *Does this music make you feel like dancing?*

Music

○ Provide a real banjo for children to explore.

Science

○ Place a small toy in a pie pan and completely cover it with water. Freeze. Place the frozen pan outdoors in the sun or in a sunny window. Invite the children to watch the water melt. *Can you guess which toy is inside the pan?* Remind the children of the line in the song that says "the sun so hot I froze to death." *Can things stay frozen in the sun?*

Snack

○ Invite the children to help make buckwheat pancakes for snack.

Writing

○ Trace magnetic letters on index cards to spell out *Susanna*. Encourage the children to place magnetic letters on top of the signs.

○ Make a Name Puzzle. Print *Susanna* on 4" x 12" strips of poster board leaving space between each letter to allow a puzzle cut. Laminate. Cut the letters apart using a puzzle cut. Encourage the children to put the name puzzle together.

Home Connection

○ Check for a family member who might play the banjo. Invite them to play for the children.

SONGS AND ACTIVITIES

Red River Valley

From this valley they say you are going.
We will miss your bright eyes and sweet smile.
For they say you are taking the sunshine
That has brightened our path for a while.

Come and sit by my side if you love me.
Do not hasten to bid me adieu,
But remember the Red River Valley
And the girl who has loved you so true.

Oh remember the Red River Valley
And the girl who has loved you so true.

Vocabulary

adieu   remember
bid   smile
bright   sunshine
hasten   valley
path
Red River Valley

Theme Connections

Friends and Families

Did You Know?

○ "Red River Valley" was originally called, "In the Bright Mohawk Valley," a tune popular in New York. It spread throughout the country and cowboys in the Red River Valley changed it to become the tune we sing today. The original song was written by James Kerrigan in 1896.

○ There are several "Red Rivers" in North America. One flows northward through the Red River Valley, forming much of the border between Minnesota and North Dakota, and then flowing into Manitoba, Canada. The Red River is 877 km long, falling 70m on its trip towards Lake Winnipeg, spreading into the vast deltaic wetland known as Netley Marsh. It was a key river in the early settlement of Canada, notably being home to the Red River Colony that later became Winnipeg.

○ In the United States, this one is called the Red River of the North, to distinguish it from another Red River (a tributary of the Mississippi River that forms part of the border between Texas and Oklahoma).

Literacy Links

Oral Language

○ Teach the children the American Sign Language sign for *goodbye* and for *I love you* (page 120-121).

Oral Language/Phonological Awareness

○ Discuss the meaning of *adieu*, which is a French word. *What are some ways of saying goodbye in English?* For example, *so long, farewell,* and *see you later.* Teach the children to say goodbye in other languages: Spanish—*adios,* Italian—*ciao,* Danish—*farvel,* Japanese—*sayonara,* and so on.

Phonological Awareness

○ Invite the children to think of words that rhyme with *red*.

○ Print *Red River* on chart paper. Ask children to identify the first letter in each word. Say the words together emphasizing the beginning sound of each word. *What sound do you hear repeated?* Tell the children that when a letter sound is repeated in a series of words it is called *alliteration*.

Curriculum Connections

Art

○ Provide paper, paintbrushes, and red, green, and blue paint. Have the children paint mountains and a river.

Blocks

○ Provide pieces of blue and green fabric to represent the river and the land. Provide newspaper or old paper sacks. Help the children create a Red River Valley. They can wad up the newspaper to place under the green fabric to make hills or mountains and then lay the blue fabric between the hills or mountains to make the river.

Discovery

○ Encourage the children to look in a mirror to determine the color of their eyes. *Do you think your eyes are bright? Why? What makes a person's eyes bright?* Encourage the children to practice smiling sweetly. *Is there more than one kind of smile? What is a sweet smile?*

> **Special Needs Adaptations:** For children with motor or vision problems, provide a hand-held mirror for them to hold close to their faces. For children who may have difficulty understanding *how* to determine the color of their eyes, model how to do it. It may be necessary to look at some pictures together, to talk about eyes and how eye color is determined. For a child with severe language delays, or those who have cognitive delays, learning to say or to sign, "My eyes are _____ (insert eye color)" will help them, as they learn to assign attributes to themselves.

Book Corner

Language

○ Provide a flannel board and facial features cut from felt. Make several different colors of eyes or use wiggle eyes with sandpaper glued onto their backs to make them stick. Encourage the children to build a face. Talk with them about their choice of features.

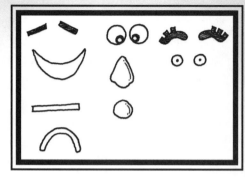

Snack

○ Invite the children to follow the Smiling Pizza Face Rebus Recipe (page 118) to make their snack.

 English Language Learner Strategy: Using a rebus makes it easier for English language learners to follow the directions.

Social Studies

○ Display a globe or map. Point out the labels of countries, states, oceans, lakes, and rivers. Point out the location of the Red River Valley (North Dakota).

Water and Sand Play

○ Provide red clay. Encourage the children to create a red river by shaping the clay to hold water.

Writing

○ Print the letter *I* on an index card. Draw an eye under the letter. Print *love* on a second card. Place a heart under the word. On a third card, print *you* and a letter U or a hand with a finger pointed outward under the word. The children can use the cards to say "I love you."

Home Connection

○ Suggest that the children ask a family member to help check the eye color of each family member and record their findings. Have the children decide which eye color is most common in their family.

Doodle-Li-Do

Vocabulary

doodle
melody
simplest
toot
waddle
wherever

Theme Connections

Movement
Music

Please sing to me that sweet melody
Called the doodle-li-do, doodle-li-do.
I like the rest but the part I like best
Goes doodle-li-do, doodle-li-do.
It's the simplest thing
There isn't much to it.
All you gotta do is doodle-li-do it.
I like it so, wherever I go.
It's a doodle-li, doodle-li-do.
Come… on… and…
Waddle-li-atcha, waddle-li-atcha,
Waddle-li-o, waddle-li-o.
Waddle-li-atcha, waddle-li-atcha,
Waddle-li-o, waddle-li-o.
It's the simplest thing
There isn't much to it.
All you gotta do is doodle-li-do it.
I like it so, wherever I go.
It's a doodle-li, doodle-li-do.
Toot! Toot!

Did You Know?

❍ "Doodle-Li-Do" is a popular camp song.
❍ The definition of doodle is to draw aimlessly. It also means to waste time.

Literacy Links

Phonological Awareness

❍ Discuss the nonsense words in the song, *waddle-li-atcha* and *doodle-li-do.* Help the children brainstorm other nonsense words, for example, *willy nilly, tweedli-dee,* and *hullabaloo.*
❍ Sing the song eliminating the initial /d/ sound in *doodle-li-do.* In other words sing *oodle-li-oo.*

Print Awareness

❍ Print "doodle-li-do" on chart paper. Ask the children to identify the letters in the word. *Which letter shows up twice? Which letters show up three times?*

Curriculum Connections

Art

❍ Doodle on sheets of drawing paper. Invite the children to make a design from the doodle.

❍ Invite the children to marble paint. Place a sheet of drawing paper in a shallow box or cake pan. Drop a marble in a cup of paint and then onto the paper. Roll the box and watch the marble make its design. Discuss the doodle design the marbles make.

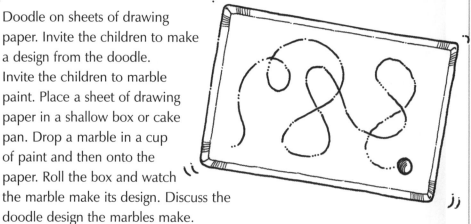

Dramatic Play

❍ Provide a pretend microphone (a toilet paper tube works well). Invite the children to sing sweet melodies.

Fine Motor

❍ Provide playdough. Encourage the children to roll snakes and then create a doodle with their snakes.

Listening

❍ Provide some of the children's favorite songs on tapes and invite the children to sing along to the melodies.

Math

❍ Doodle on index cards. Make five doodles on the first card, four on the next, three on the next, then two, and finally one. Provide numerals from 1-5 and invite the children to place the numeral that corresponds to the number of doodles on the card beside the card.

Music and Movement

❍ Invite the children to create new hand motions for the song.

(✓) **Special Needs Adaptation:** Look for ways for children with special needs to participate, such as shaking a tambourine while others sing, using a scarf to dance with the music, and tapping or playing a pretend drum while others complete more complicated hand-movements. Invite children to tap or slap their thighs, while others do hand-movements. Playing spoons (using spoons to make music) is an old tradition, which can be adapted for children with special needs. Use large spoons and model how to hold a spoon in each hand and hit the backs together to make a noise in time with the music.

Campfire Songs by Irene Maddox
D Is for Doodle by Deborah Zemke
Sing-Along Song by JoAnn Early Macken

Snack

❍ Invite the children to help make Snicker Doodles (page 106) for snack. *Why do people call these cookies Snicker Doodles?*

Writing

❍ Print *doodle-li-do* on chart paper. Provide a tray of sand and invite the children to doodle in the sand. Challenge them to use their index fingers to write *doodle-li-do* in the sand.

Home Connection

❍ Send doodles home with every child. Ask families to create something from the doodle and return it to school. Have a show-and-tell session or create a bulletin board.

I've Been Riding on the Range by Richele Bartkowiak

(Tune: I've Been Working on the Railroad)
I've been riding on the range,
All the livelong day.
I've been riding on the range,
Herding dogies on their way.

Can't you hear the cowboys shouting,
"Yippity-oh-ky-yay!"
Can't you hear the cowboys shouting,
"Dogies, move this way!"

Dogies won't you move, dogies won't you move,
Dogies won't you move this way, this way?
Dogies won't you move, dogies won't you move,
Dogies won't you move this way?

Someone's out herdin' those dogies.
Someone's herdin' today.
Someone's out herdin' those dogies.
Singin' "Dogies move this way!"

Let's sing it
Yippity, yippity-oh-ky-yay,
Yippity-oh-ky-yay.
Yippity, yippity-oh-ky-yay,
Strumming on the old banjo!

Vocabulary

cowboy
dogies
herding
livelong
move
range

Theme Connections

Animals
Sounds

Did You Know?
- Each piece of cowboy attire plays a role in the work of the cowboy.
- The cowboy kerchief or bandana is essential. It is used as a dust mask while driving cattle that kick up dirt, as earmuffs in cold weather, as protection from sunburn on the neck, as a potholder for hot pots or branding irons, as prevention against snow blindness in winter, and as a tourniquet or sling in case of injury. Bandanas are often the color red; the

material can be silk, cotton, or linen. Even today, the bandana is generally folded into a triangle and tied around the neck, but with the knot in the back.

○ Boots with pointy toes and high heels were designed and preferred because of their performance in the saddle. The heels allowed a good grip in the stirrup and the pointy toes allowed for fluid movement in and out of the stirrup.

○ Chaps, pronounced correctly as "shaps," is short for chaparejos (shap-ar-EH-hos), which is another important cowboy tool. These leather britches or wrap-around leggings are worn to prevent injury to the legs while chasing cattle. Popular types of chaps are woollies and shotguns.

○ The hat is often a Stetson hat, but it always has a high crown and a wide brim. The cowboy hat was originally created for Buffalo Bill Cody, who wanted a larger-than-life cowboy hat for his Wild West Show. And contrary to the name, the hat could not hold 10-gallons of anything.

○ A dogie is a motherless calf.

○ The first Texas trail drives were short trips, but when short routes became unprofitable, the long trail rides began.

○ See pages 30-31 for more information about trail rides.

Literacy Links

Comprehension
○ Invite the children to participate in the action story "Going on a Trail Ride" (page 104).

Letter Knowledge
○ Print *yippity* on chart paper. Ask volunteers to identity the letters. Count the number of each letter in the word. *Which letter is the only letter that appears once?*

Oral Language
○ Discuss cattle drives. *Where do the cowboys take the cattle? What do the cowboys wear? How do they herd the cattle?*

○ Teach the children the American Sign Language sign for *cattle* (page 120).

Curriculum Connections

Art

❍ Cut an old white sheet into 18" squares. Provide two or three tubes of dye and rubber bands. Give each child a square of sheet. Show the children how to use rubber bands to section off their square and then dip it in the color or colors of dye they want to use for their bandana. Talk with the children as they work. *Why do cowboys wear bandanas?*

Blocks

❍ Provide a square of green and a square of brown fabric for the children to use as "the range" groundcover. Provide plastic horses, cows, cowboys, and cowgirls. Invite the children to pretend they are herding cattle across the range.

Games

❍ Make two photocopies of the Western Patterns (page 112). Color them, cut them out, and laminate them. Use the cards to play Western Concentration.

❍ Make a Cowboy Dice Game. Make five photocopies of the cowboy pattern (page 111). Color them and laminate them. Cut three of the copies into six whole item puzzle pieces. For example, cut out the hat, the face, the shirt (with hands attached), the pants, bandanas, and the boots. Glue one set of parts on a pint milk carton that has been folded into a square and covered with white paper to make a game die. Give each child an intact copy of a cowboy and a set of cowboy puzzle pieces to be used to lie on top of the intact copy. Have the children roll the die and place the item that they roll on top of their copy. If they land on something they have already placed on their cowboy, they miss a turn. The first child to cover all the parts wins the game.

✔ **Special Needs Adaptation:** Make two copies of the cowboy and color each one using the same colors (for example, the boots on both copies would be the same color). Leave one copy intact and cut out the clothing on the other copy (for example, cut out the hat, face, shirt with hands attached, pants, bandana, and the boots). With no more than two children, talk about the various items of clothing the cowboy could wear. Hold up each piece as you talk about it. After discussing a specific piece of clothing, invite a child to place the item on top of the copy. Continue, until each child has a turn.

Language

○ Make two or three photocopies of the Western Brands (page 107). Cut them out and laminate them. Invite the children to match the brands.

○ Make Cowboy Puzzles. Make photocopies of the cowboy pattern (page 111). Color the copies, laminate them, and then cut them into puzzle pieces. Invite the children to work the puzzles. Talk with the children about how the pieces fit together.

Snack

○ Invite the children to follow the Trail Mix Rebus Recipe (page 119) to make their snack. **Allergy Warning:** Check for peanut allergies.

 English Language Learner Strategy: Using a rebus makes it easier for English language learners to follow the directions.

Writing

○ Provide examples of brands. Challenge the children to use markers and paper to create their own brand or, if they prefer, to copy the brands you have provided.

Home Connection

○ Suggest that families watch a Western movie together.

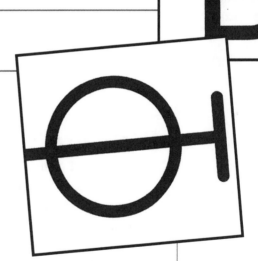

Cowboys by Lucille Recht Penner
The Dirty Cowboy by Amy Timberlake
I Want to Be a Cowboy by Dan Liebman

Look Around the Prairie by Pam Schiller

(Tune: Did You Ever See a Lassie?)
Chorus:
Oh, look around the prairie,
The prairie, the prairie.
Oh, look around the prairie.
Now what do you see?

Oh, I see some sand!
Yes, I see some sand!
Oh, look around the prairie
Now what do you see?

(Chorus)

Oh, I see a lizard!
Yes, I see a lizard!
Oh, look around the prairie
Now what do you see?

(Chorus)

Oh, I see a cactus!
Yes, I see a cactus!
Oh, look around the prairie
Now what do you see?

(Chorus)

Oh, I see a snake!
Yes, I see a snake!
Oh, look around the prairie
Now what do you see?

Oh, look around the prairie,
The prairie, the prairie.
Yes, look around the prairie
There's so much to see!

Vocabulary

bison
grass
hawk
look
prairie
prairie dog

Theme Connections

Animals

Did You Know?

❍ While most prairies are characterized by grasses, there are other types of prairies including sand prairies, gravel prairies, and hill prairies. Grassland prairies are divided into three categories—tall grass prairies, mixed grass prairies, and short grass prairies.

❍ Tall grass prairie once covered 142 million acres in the United States—covering about 40% of the country.

❍ Prairies are one of the most recently developed ecosystems in North America. Prairies formed about 8,000 years ago. Over 100 plant species can occur on a prairie in less than five acres. About one percent of the original North American prairies still exist.

❍ Up to 60 million bison grazed on the plains and prairies of North America when European explorers first arrived and fewer than 600 existed by 1885.

❍ Grazing is an integral part of the prairie ecosystem and increases the growth of prairie plants.

○ A bison can consume 30-50 pounds of feed each day. Prairie dogs gravitate to the patches of close-cropped grass left by grazing bison where they can watch for prowling predators.

○ Prairie wildlife includes bison, bobcats, gophers, snakes, earthworms, jack rabbits, deer, antelope, badgers, mountain lions, grasshoppers, scorpions, and ants. Prairie dogs increase the populations of other prairie wildlife, such as hawks, foxes, and ferrets, which are all predators of the prairie dog.

○ Prior to pioneer settlement, some five billion prairie dogs in extensive colonies spread across hundreds of miles of prairie.

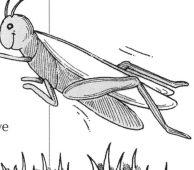

Literacy Links

Letter Knowledge

○ Print *prairie* on chart paper. Have the children identify the first letter. *Which letters show up two times in prairie?*

Oral Language

○ Display photos of prairies. Discuss life in the prairie. *Who lives there? What is the weather like? How is it different from living in the mountains?* Discuss prairie animals. Challenge children to write a new verse to the song.

○ Ask a volunteer to use *prairie* in a sentence.

Phonological Awareness

○ Challenge the children to think of words that rhyme with prairie (scary, cherry, berry). Challenge the children to think of names that rhyme with prairie (Harry, Mary, Terry, Larry, Barry).

Curriculum Connections

Art

○ Tape a six- to eight-foot sheet of white butcher paper or bulletin board paper to the wall. Provide several shades of green tempera paint, along with yellow and brown tempera paint. Encourage the children to paint a tall grass prairie on the butcher paper or bulletin board paper.

Dramatic Play

○ Provide props for a prairie setting, such as pots and pans, playdough for making bread, a washboard for washing clothes, quilts, and so on. Encourage the children to pretend they are living on the prairie. This activity will need some adult participation because children may have very little reference for prairie living.

Fine Motor

○ Provide green and brown playdough. Encourage the children to roll the dough to make prairie snakes.

Math

○ Cut several five foot pieces of green yarn to represent the length of tall prairie grass. Cut several two foot pieces of yarn to represent the length of short prairie grass. Have the children use the pieces of yarn to find things in the classroom that are both lengths.

> ✔ **Special Needs Adaptation:** Use a single length of yarn and demonstrate how to measure with it. Provide several items to measure or direct the child to specific items that you know are the same size as his length of yarn. For children who may be limited by mobility or in a wheelchair, provide a smaller length of yarn and five items (two or three that are the same size as his yarn and two or three that are either longer or shorter than his yarn). Encourage the child to measure the items you have selected. For a child with language delays, model the language to use, such as, "Marcus, the block is the same length as your rope" or "Lakisha, the truck is longer than your rope."

Sand and Water Play

○ Provide a shallow tub of sand, small rocks to make hills, and paper grass. Invite the children to make a prairie. Provide plastic prairie animals to add to the scene.

Science

○ Invite the children to plant rye grass in a Styrofoam cup of potting soil. When the grass starts to sprout, place the cups together to make a prairie.
○ Provide photos of prairie animals, including insects and reptiles. Have the children sort the animals by the number of legs each animal has.

Special Needs Adaptation: Talk about the pictures of the prairie animals. Instead of sorting by the number of legs, try sorting by size (big and small) or talk about how the animal looks, what it eats, or what kind of "house" it lives in.

Snack

○ Provide graham crackers, pretzels, peanut butter, cereal squares, and mini candy-coated chocolate pieces. Encourage the children to follow the Prairie Home Rebus Recipe (page 117) to make a Prairie Home Snack. **Allergy Warning:** Check for peanut allergies.

 English Language Learner Strategy: Using a rebus makes it easier for English language learners to follow the directions.

Home Connection

○ Have the children take a five-foot strip of green yarn home with them. Challenge them to find something inside or outside at home that is five feet long.

Polly Wolly Doodle

Oh, I went down South for to see my Sal.
Singing Polly wolly doodle all the day.
My Sal, she is a spunky gal,
Singing Polly wolly doodle all the day.

Chorus:
Fare thee well, fare thee well,
Fare thee well my fairy fay.
For I'm going to Lou'siana for to see my Susyanna,
Singing Polly wolly doodle all the day.

Oh, my Sal, she is a maiden fair.
Singing Polly wolly doodle all the day.
With curly eyes and laughing hair,
Singing Polly wolly doodle all the day.

(Chorus)

Behind the barn, down on my knees,
Singing Polly wolly doodle all the day.
I thought I heard a chicken sneeze.
Singing Polly wolly doodle all the day.

(Chorus)

He sneezed so hard with the whooping cough.
Singing Polly wolly doodle all the day.
He sneezed his head and the tail right off.
Singing Polly wolly doodle all the day.

(Chorus)

A grasshopper on a railroad track.
Singing Polly wolly doodle all the day.
Pickin' his teeth with a carpet tack.
Singing Polly wolly doodle all the day.

(Chorus)

Vocabulary

barn
carpet tack
chicken
curly
fair
fare thee well
gal
grasshopper
maiden
railroad track
sneeze
South
spunky
whooping cough

Theme Connections

Animals
Humor
Movement
Music

Did You Know?

○ "Polly-Wolly-Doodle" is a popular camp song.

○ "Polly-Wolly-Doodle" was introduced by Daniel Decatur Emmett's Virginia Minstrels in the 1840s and is still a popular children's song today. The origin of the song is unknown, but it may well have its origins as a song sung by slaves in the south.

Literacy Links

Oral Language

○ Show the children a carpet tack. Point out how sharp it is. Ask the children to suggest other things that the grasshopper could use to pick his teeth.

○ Discuss the humorous lines in the song; for example, "I thought I heard a chicken sneeze" or "pickin' his teeth with a carpet tack."

○ Discuss sneezing and teeth-picking etiquette.

Phonological Awareness

○ Have the children say *polly wolly* several times. Encourage them to think of other words that rhyme with *polly* and *wolly. What does* polly wolly doodle *mean?*

○ Sing the song substituting *willy nilly noodle* for *polly wolly doodle.*

Phonological Awareness/Letter Knowledge

○ Print *polly wolly* on chart paper. Ask the children to identify the first letter in each word. Point out that the two words rhyme. Print a second pair of rhyming words; for example, *willy nilly.* Point out that in both sets of rhyming words it is only the first letter that is different. Make up a third rhyming word for each pair of words, perhaps molly for the first set and silly for the second set. Point out that once again it is only the first letter that is different in each word.

Print Awareness

○ Help the children make a list of different ways that people say goodbye, for example, so long, farewell, adios, see you later, ciao, and so on.

Curriculum Connections

Construction

○ Make Sal Puppets. Give each child a six inch paper plate and tongue depressor. Provide yarn, paper ribbon, markers, wiggle eyes, and construction paper. Show the children how to curl the paper ribbon to make curly lashes for their puppet. Unravel pieces of yarn to make laughing hair. When the children are finished with their Sal's face have them glue it to the tongue depressor to make a puppet.

 Special Needs Adaptation: Invite a peer buddy to help the child with special needs construct his puppet, according to his directions. Some children may be able to help make a puppet, but will have difficulty grasping a tongue depressor. Cover the depressor with cloth or make it thicker by gluing three or more of the sticks together. This provides a larger surface for the child to grasp.

Fine Motor

○ Roll playdough in birdseed. Provide toothpicks for the children to use to pick seeds from playdough. Remind them of the grasshopper in the song who used a carpet tack to pick his teeth. *What do you think was stuck in the grasshopper's teeth?*

Games

○ Play Polly Wolly Volley. Show the children how to toss a soft ball (such as a Nerf ball) into the air and then work with a partner to keep the ball up in the air by volleying it.

Special Needs Adaptation: Roll or throw a soft ball back and forth while you sing or hum the song.

Gross Motor

○ Teach the children how to do Grasshopper Jumps. Place a strip of masking tape on the floor to represent a jump line. Have the children squat and then jump. Place a marker where they land. Who makes the longest jump?

Outdoors

○ Play Hide and Seek. Instruct the children to substitute "oodlely-oodlely-oh" for "alli-alli-onkin" when they get to home base.

Book Corner

Cowboys by Lucille
   Recht Penner
The Dirty Cowboy by
   Amy Timberlake
*I Want to Be a
   Cowboy* by Dan
   Liebman
*Miss Polly Wolly
   Doodle from
   Tibet* by
   Beaumont

Snack

❍ Invite the children to follow the directions on the Oodles Noodles Rebus
   Recipe (page 116) to make their snack.

Social Studies

❍ Display a map or a globe. Show the children where Louisiana is. Show
   them where the Southern part of the United States is located.

Writing

❍ Print *polly wolly doodle* on index cards. Encourage the children to make
   doodles over the letters.

❍ See page 70 for additional doodle activities.

Home Connection

❍ Encourage the children to talk with their families about sneezing
   etiquette.

Five Little Cowboys

by Pam Schiller and Richele Bartkowiak

Five little cowboys sitting on a gate.
The 1st one said," This rodeo's great!"
The 2nd one said," I love the clowns."
The 3rd one said, "I like the sounds."
The 4th one said, "Can you ride a bull?"
The 5th one said," No, but it sure looks cool!"
Then buzz went the bell and the gate flew open
And off went the cowboys ridin' and ropin'.

✓ **Special Needs Adaptation:** This song is a great opportunity to practice the concepts of 1-5. Cut five sheets of poster board in half, and write the numerals 1-5 on them, giving you two half-sheets of poster board with the number 1, two with the number 2, and so on. Punch a hole in the top of each half-sheet and insert a length of yarn to attach the two halves. Tie a knot so that the half-sheets of poster board can be hung across a child's shoulder. Assign one child to be number 1, one to be number 2, and so on. Use to act out the song, with each child standing when his number is sung in the song.

Vocabulary

bell
bull
buzz
clowns
cowboy
gate
ridin'
rodeo
ropin'

Theme Connections

Animals
Counting
Sounds

Did You Know?

❍ The rodeo is a traditional North American folk sport with influences from the history of Mexican *vaqueros* and American cowboys.

❍ Rodeo events include the rough stock events: bull riding, bareback bronco riding, saddle bronco riding, plus the timed events: steer wrestling, team roping, calf roping, the rarely seen steer roping, and women's barrel racing, breakaway roping, goat roping, and pole bending.

❍ The participants include cowboys, cowgirls, and also rodeo clowns or bull fighters.

Literacy Links

Comprehension

○ Appoint children to represent each of the five cowboys. Invite the children to act out the rhyme.

○ Make a Cowboy Glove Puppet. Photocopy the Cowboy pattern (page 112). Make five copies of the Cowboy pattern. Color them, cut them out, and laminate them. Glue Velcro to the back of each cowboy. Glue the opposite piece of Velcro on each finger of a work glove. Stick the puppets on the glove fingers to make a Cowboy Glove Puppet. Use the puppet with the chant on the previous page.

Oral Language

○ Discuss the treats that are found at the rodeo, for example, popcorn, peanuts, cotton candy, and snow cones. *Which treat would you choose?*

○ Teach the children the American Sign Language sign for *cowboy* (page 120).

Curriculum Connections

Blocks

○ Help the children build a rodeo arena with the blocks. Provide plastic horses, cows, and cowboys and cowgirls. Encourage the children to pretend they are at a rodeo.

Dramatic Play

○ Provide clown attire and a mirror. Invite the children to dress as rodeo clowns.

Fine Motor

○ Teach the children how to tie simple knots.

○ Provide peanuts and encourage the children to shell and eat them. Talk with the children about the other treats available at the rodeo. (**Allergy Warning:** Check for peanut allergies.)

Games

○ Make a Cowboy Dice Game. Make five photocopies of the Cowboy (page 111). Color them and laminate them. Cut three of the copies into whole item puzzle pieces. For example, cut out the hat, the face, the shirt (with hands attached), the pants, bandanas, and the boots. Glue one set

SONGS AND ACTIVITIES

Book Corner

Cowboy Counting by Ann Herbert Scott
Cowboys by Lucille Recht Penner
The Dirty Cowboy by Amy Timberlake
I Want to Be a Cowboy by Dan Liebman

of parts on a pint milk carton that has been folded into a square and covered with white paper to make a game die. Give each child an intact copy of a Cowboy and a set of cowboy puzzle pieces to be used to lie on top of the intact copy. Have the children roll the die and place the item that they roll on top of their copy. If they land on something they have already placed on their copy they miss a turn. The first child to cover all the parts wins the game.

Gross Motor

❍ Cut 36″ lengths of rope. Tie each strip in a circle. Lay the ropes on the floor about a foot apart in a trail or pathway. Challenge the children to jump from rope circle to rope circle along the path.

Language

❍ Encourage the children to use the Cowboy Glove Puppet (see Literacy Links) to retell the chant.

Writing

❍ Print *rodeo* on index cards. Provide small pieces of rope for the children to use to glue over the letters.

❍ See pages 90-92 in "One Rodeo Clown" for additional activities.

Home Connection

❍ Encourage the children to teach their families the song as a fingerplay.

Let's Go Riding

Vocabulary

riding
saddle
giddy-up

Theme Connections

Animals

(Tune: Are You Sleeping?)
Lets go riding, lets go riding,
Saddle up. Saddle up.
Everybody ready? Everybody ready?
Giddy-up! Giddy-up!
(Repeat)

Did You Know?

○ Horse riding is called *equestrianism*.
  Equestrianism includes both riding horses for practical purposes, such as
  in police work or for controlling herd animals on a ranch, as well as for
  recreation and sport, such as horse riding sports, dressage, show
  jumping, "eventing," and polo. Other horse riding activities include
  horse-racing, hunting, fox hunting, rodeo, endurance, jousting, and
  cavalry. Horses are often used for recreational rides, which many parks
  and ranches offer to visitors.

○ Horse riding and equestrian activities involve various techniques for
  controlling a horse's gait, speed, and direction as well as a familiarity
  with equine equipment, or tack, and horse training and grooming. The
  introduction of the harness and other controlling devices contributed
  greatly to the development of different riding styles and the use of horses.

○ Equestrian competitions can be traced back to the early Olympic Games.
  Many horse events are held on local, regional, and national levels every
  year throughout the world.

Literacy Links

Comprehension

○ Invite the children to participate in the action story, "Let's Go on a Trail
  Ride" (page 105). Discuss the things one has to do to get ready for the
  ride.

Horse

Listening

❍ Read the listening story, "Quinn and Dusty" (page 105). Have the children call out *yippee* every time you say, "Quinn," and call out *giddy-up* every time you say, "Dusty."

Oral Language

❍ Discuss horse riding. *What equipment (tack) do you need to ride? Where does the saddle go? Why do you need a saddle when you ride? Why do you need a bridle and reins?* Discuss the vocabulary used to get a horse to move (giddy up) and to stop (whoa).

❍ Teach the children the American Sign Language sign for *horse* (page 121).

Curriculum Connections

Blocks

❍ Invite the children to build a barn and some horse pens. Provide plastic horses for dramatic play.

> **Special Needs Adaptation:** Reinforce collaboration and cooperative play. Help the child with special needs participate by giving him a specific task to accomplish, such as putting the horses in the pen or helping close the horse pen. Monitor group play and look for ways to encourage everyone to participate in some way. If the child is hesitant to participate, suggest that you and the child do it together. For example, you could put a horse in the pen, and then invite the child to put his horse in the pen.

Discovery

❍ Provide a saddle and bridle for children to explore.

Games

❍ Invite the children to play Trail Ride. Make a game board by drawing a trail (with game square spaces) from the top left corner of the board to the bottom right corner. Use pictures from the Western Patterns (page 112) to decorate the board if desired. Draw a small town around the start line at the top of the board and another small town at the bottom by the finish line. Color the game space squares in a pattern of red, yellow and green. Provide 27 playing cards with red, yellow, and green dots on them. Add three cards to the playing cards that have no dots to make a deck of 30 cards. Make two horse and wagon game pieces by attaching the bottom of a small matchbox to a plastic horse with string. Have the children move their horse and wagon along the trail by

Giddy Up! Let's Ride!
by Flora
Mcdonnell
Pony Rider by Edna
Walker Chandler
The Sleep Ponies by
Gudrun Ongman

drawing a playing card and moving to the next square of the color they have drawn. If they draw a card with no colored dot they must loose a turn. The first wagon that reaches the finish line wins.

Gross Motor

○ Provide wrapping paper tubes for children to use as stick horses. Use masking tape to make a trail on the floor for children to follow.

Listening

○ Provide drumsticks and cardboard boxes, plastic tubs, and buckets. Encourage the children to tap the drumsticks on the various surfaces to create the sound of a horse trotting.

Movement

○ Teach the children to gallop and prance like a horse. When outdoors, encourage the children to have a galloping race.

Snack/Math

○ Invite the children to help make Cowboy Punch. Mix ½ gallon of lemonade with ½ gallon of grape juice. Provide a small ladle (gravy ladle or ¼ cup measuring cup), a small pitcher, and six-ounce paper cups. *How many ladles does it take to fill the pitcher? How many ladles does it take to fill the cup?*

Home Connection

○ Suggest that the children look at home for western items. *Does someone have a cowboy hat? What about boots? Is there a ladle in the kitchen?*

One Rodeo Clown

by Pam Schiller

(Tune: One Elephant)
One funny clown
Went out to play
In the arena on rodeo day.
He had such outrageous fun
He called for another
Funny clown to come.

Additional verses:
Two funny clowns…
Three funny clowns…
Four funny clowns…
Five funny clowns…

Vocabulary

arena
clown
funny
outrageous
rodeo

Theme Connections

Clowns
Workers

Did You Know?

❍ Rodeo clowns are sometimes called *barrelmen*.
❍ A barrelman is one of the brightly costumed clowns highly visible in rodeo arenas throughout most performances and particularly during events like bull riding. A barrelman's job is to entertain the crowd with comedy skits and/or jokes during a rodeo's inevitable down time. As part of his act, the barrelman hangs around a custom-made barrel, which he uses (among other things) to protect himself from charging bulls.
❍ See page 37 in "The Rodeo" for more information about rodeo clowns.

Literacy Links

Oral Language

❍ Sing the song again changing *funny* for another descriptive word with two syllables such as jolly, silly, saggy, laughing, and so on.
❍ Discuss clown costumes and behaviors. *What do clowns do to their face? Why do they where big clothes and big shoes? What makes the clown funny?*

Phonological Awareness
○ Have the children think of words that rhyme with *clown*.

Curriculum Connections

Art
○ Invite the children to help mix face paint. Place 2 tablespoons of cold cream, ½ teaspoon of glycerin, 1 teaspoon of cornstarch. and 1 teaspoon of dry tempera in a small mixing bowl. Stir together until well mixed. Encourage the children to try some face paint on the back side of their hands. (**Caution:** Do not allow children to paint on their faces without permission from their family)
○ Provide red and white tempera paint. Invite the children to experiment making clown smiles. Show them how to make big smiles and small smiles and how to make happy smiles and frowns.

Games
○ Play You Can't Make Me Laugh. Have the children sit on the floor in a circle. Select one child to be the clown. Challenge the clown to stand in the middle of the circle and do funny antics in an attempt to make the children laugh. When the clown is successful, have her choose a classmate to replace her as the clown.
○ Invite the children to play Clown in the Barrel. Paint clown faces on ping pong balls. Provide a coffee can for a barrel. Encourage the children to attempt to toss or bounce the clown heads into the barrel.

✔ **Special Needs Adaptation:** Adapt for children with motor difficulty by using tennis balls or other large balls and by using a bucket or large box for a barrel instead of a coffee can.

Language
○ Make photocopies of the Clown Rhyming Word Cards (page 108) and the Rose Rhyming Word Cards (page 109). Color them, cut them out, and laminate them. Give both sets of cards to the children and have them identify the ones that rhyme with clown.
○ Cut a clown face and a variety of facial features from felt. Provide lengths of red and gold yarn to use for hair. Provide a flannel board and encourage the children to create clown faces.

Book Corner

Ollie Jolly, Rodeo Clown by Jo Harper

Rodeo Clown: Laughs and Danger in the Ring by Keith Elliot Greenberg

Rodeo Time by Stuart Murphy

✓ **Special Needs Adaptation:** Model how to use the felt pieces to make a funny clown. Later, ask questions to help him make his own clown. For example, say, "Make his eyes funny" or "Show me a funny clown smile." For children with very limited vocabulary, use the activity as an opportunity to reinforce the child's knowledge of the parts of the body. For example, you might make a funny clown face from the felt pieces and ask the child to "Point to the clown's eyes" or "Show me the clown's mouth."

Movement

❍ Encourage the children to dance a funny clown dance between a light source and the wall to create humorous shadow clowns.

Snack

❍ Make Clown Face Toast. Toast English muffins. Give each child half a muffin for a face. Mix pineapple juice with cream cheese to create white face paint and cherry juice with cream cheese to create pink face paint. Encourage the children to ice their muffin face. Provide cherries, tangerine slices, string licorice, grated carrot, miniature marshmallow, nuts, and small candies. Allow children to create clown faces. **Allergy Warning:** Check for allergies.

Home Connection

❍ Send a set of Clown Rhyming Word Cards (page 108) home for the children to show their parents the many things that rhyme with clown.

Ram, Sam, Sam: Western Style

Vocabulary

bucking bull
calf
giggly
laughing
rodeo
rowdy
silly

Theme Connections

Animals
Humor
Sounds

Did You Know?

○ See pages 37 and 90 for information about rodeos.

A ram sam sam
A ram sam sam
Goolie, goolie, goolie, goolie, goolie
Ram sam sam
A raffy, a raffy
Goolie, goolie, goolie, goolie, goolie
Ram sam sam

A rodeo clown
A rodeo clown
Goolie, goolie, goolie, goolie, goolie
Rodeo clown
A funny, a funny
Goolie, goolie, goolie, goolie, goolie
Rodeo clown!

(Other verses):
A bucking bull…a rowdy…
A baby calf…a silly…
A laughing child…a giggly…

(Repeat first verse.)

Literacy Links

Letter Knowledge
○ Print *Ram, Sam, Sam* on chart paper. Ask children to identify the word that starts with a different letter. *Which letters are in all three words?*

Oral Language

○ Following the western theme add new verses to the song, for example, a sticky cactus, flying hawk, running horse and so on.

Special Needs Adaptation: Make a box of words that relate to the West (for example, cowboy, rodeo, cattle, horse, saddle, cactus, West, hat, boots, spurs, and so on). Paste a picture on each card above the word. Whenever possible, bring in real objects as well, such as a small cactus, a pair of boots, a western hat, and, if possible, a saddle. Talk about the pictures and the items. Encourage the children to use each one in a sentence. For a child who is non-verbal, see if he will point to the item when you name it. After several days, repeat the activity. Some children with special needs have difficulty retaining new information. It may be necessary to repeat this activity several times.

Phonological Awareness

○ Point out the *alliteration* (repetition of consonant sounds) in goolie, goolie, goolie. Print *Ram Sam Sam* on chart paper. Ask the children to identify the first letter in each word. *Which word has a different first letter?* Ask the children to think of another word that rhymes with *ram* and *Sam*. Sing the song with new rhyming words; for example, *Pam, bam, bam.*

Curriculum Connections

Art

○ Invite the children to draw a Western picture.

Fine Motor

○ Provide monofilament, cut into one-inch strips to represent cactus spines, and tweezers. Challenge children to pick up the spines with the tweezers and move them from one bowl to another.

○ Photocopy and enlarge the Western Patterns (page 112) to make Western Puzzles. Color them, cut them out, and laminate them. Cut them into puzzle pieces and allow children to work the puzzles. Put colored dots on the back of puzzle pieces to identify the pieces that belong to each puzzle.

Games

○ Make photocopies of the Western Patterns (page 112). Color them, cut them out, and laminate them. Give them to the children and invite them to play Western Concentration.

○ Encourage children to play the Barrel Race Game. Cut out two-inch squares of red construction paper and tape them to a tabletop around a coffee can that represents the barrel of the barrel races. Write *start* on one square to mark the beginning of the track. Give the children plastic horses and a die. Invite them to roll the die and move their horses along the track to the barrel the number of squares indicated. The first horse around the barrel wins the race.

Language

○ Photocopy the Clown Rhyming Word Cards (page 108) or the Rose Rhyming Word Cards (page 109). Color them, cut them out, and laminate them. Mix the sets of cards together and have the children identify the cards that rhyme with clown.

Math

○ Cut sponges into the shape of Western hats or boots or both. Provide tempera paint. Encourage the children to use the sponges and tempera paint to create Western patterns.

Writing

○ Make a box of index cards that have words on each one that relate to the West, such as cowboy, rodeo, cattle, horse, saddle, cactus, west, hat, boots, spurs, and so on. Allow the children to select words from the box and copy them.

○ Print *Ram, Sam, Sam* on chart paper. Invite the children to use magnetic letters to copy the words.

Home Connection

○ Encourage the children to sing the song with their families. Suggest that families add a new verse to the song. Have the children share their family verses when they return.

Book Corner

Cindy Ellen: A Wild Western Cinderella by Susan Lowell
The Cowboy and the Black-Eyed Pea by Tony Johnston
Cowboys by Lucille Recht Penner
Dusty Locks and the Three Bears by Susan Lowell
The Rodeo by Cheryl Walsh

SONGS AND ACTIVITIES

Turkey in the Straw

As I was a-goin' on down the road,
A tired man with a heavy load,
I called for help and a fairy winked
Said, "You'll be home in a "blink, blink, blink!"

Chorus:
Turkey in the straw, turkey in the hay.
Roll 'em up and twist 'em up
A high tuck a-haw
And hit 'em up a tune called
"Turkey in the Straw."

Went out to milk and I didn't know how
I milked the goat instead of the cow
A monkey sittin' on a pile of straw
And a laughin' bird went caw, caw, caw!

(Chorus)

I came to the river; it was mighty wide,
So I paid five dollars for a boat to ride.
Well, it wouldn't go forward and it wouldn't back,
And the water came in 'cause the floor had a crack!

(Chorus)

As I came down the new cut road,
Met Mr. Bullfrog, met Miss Toad
And every time Miss Toad would sing,
Old Mr. Bullfrog cut a pigeon wing.

(Chorus)

Did you ever go fishin' on a warm summer day
When all the fish were swimmin' in the bay
With their hands in their pockets and their pockets in their pants?
Did you ever see a fishie do the Hootchy-Kootchy Dance?

(Chorus)

Vocabulary

bird
blink
boat
bullfrog
caw
cow
crack
fairy
floor
goat
load
milk
monkey
pigeon
pocket
river
straw
toad
turkey
wide
winked

Theme Connections

Animals
Humor

Did You Know?

O "Turkey in the Straw" was one of the earliest American minstrel songs. It was a fiddle tune named "Natchez Under the Hill" before it was published with words in 1834 as "Old Zip Coon." It was very popular during Andrew Jackson's presidency.

O The first verse of the original song, "Old Zip Coon," is:

> There once was a man with a double chin
> Who performed with skill on the violin,
> And he played in time and he played in tune,
> But he wouldn't play anything but Old Zip Coon.

O The tune is reportedly derived from the ballad "My Grandmother Lived on Yonder Little Green" which was derived from the Irish ballad "The Old Rose Tree."

Literacy Links

Oral Language

O Discuss the silly things in the song such as a fairy winking, milking a goat instead of a cow, a boat with a crack, and a fish doing the Hootchy-Kootchy Dance. Have a volunteer demonstrate a fish doing the Hootchy-Kootchy.

O Discuss and demonstrate the difference between winking and blinking.

O Discuss the meaning of the phrase in the song, "cut a pigeon wing." There are several other phrases for dancing such as "cut a rug" and "trip the light fantastic." The phrase "cut a pigeon wing" also appears in "Short'nin' Bread."

Phonological Awareness

O Make a list of some of the rhyming words in the song, *road/load*, *wink/blink*, *wide/ride*, *cow/how*, and so on.

Curriculum Connections

Art

❍ Invite the children to make handprint turkeys. Provide finger paint. Have the children cover their hand in the paint and then press their hand onto a sheet of drawing paper. The thumb will be the turkey's head and the fingers will be the turkey's feathers. Use crayons or markers to add legs, an eye, and a gobbler.

✓ **Special Needs Adaptation:** If a child resists placing his hand in the paint, assist him by helping him or by sticking your hand in first. As an alternative to paint, try tracing the child's hand or outlining it with a marker.

Discovery

❍ Provide a tub of water and several items the children can test for their ability to sink or float. Provide two of each item, one item with a crack and the other not cracked. For example a Styrofoam meat tray one with a large crack in it and one without a crack in it, and in the same fashion a paper plate, a plastic egg, a cup, and so on.

Dramatic Play

❍ Cut fish from construction paper. Invite the children to glue large clear sequins (scales) on their fish. Provide a wiggle eye for the fish. Attach a fifteen-inch piece of elastic thread to each fish. Invite the children to wiggle the string to dance their fish.

Games

❍ Cut fish from construction paper. On each one of the fish print one of the letters in *turkey*. Place a paper clip on the nose of each fish. Make a fishing pole from a sturdy coat hanger tube and a string with a magnet attached to one end. Invite the children to catch the fish with the magnet. After all the fish have been caught have the children arrange them so that the letters on the fish spell turkey.

❍ Play What's in the Pant's Pocket. Place a small toy inside the pocket of a pair of western jeans. Let children take turns feeling the object first outside the pocket and then inside the pocket. Ask them to identify the object in the pocket without taking it out of the pocket.

Music and Movement

❍ Play exotic music and invite the children to create a "Hootchy-Kootchy Dance."

❍ Play banjo music and invite the children to "cut a pigeon wing."

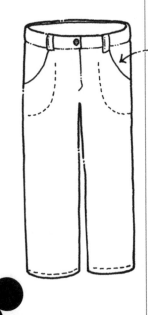

Book Corner

Barn Dance by Bill
    Martin, Jr. and
    John
    Archambault
The Dirty Cowboy by
    Amy Timberlake
Turkey in the Straw
    by Phil Rosenthal

Sand and Water Play

○ Fill the water/sand table with hay. Hide items in the hay and challenge the children to find them. If you have a plastic turkey, hide it in the hay. If you want to make the play more fun, make the search for the turkey the object of the game. Talk with children about the feel of the hay. *It is light or heavy? Is it sticky of smooth? How would you describe hay?*

✓ **Special Needs Adaptation:** Hide items that are large enough for the child to pick up. If the child has difficulty picking up items, make round handles for each item by attaching an inexpensive shower curtain ring to the top of each item. It will be much easier for the child to grasp the large ring.

Writing

○ Print *turkey* on index cards. Make a turkey foot by twisting pipe cleaners together to form three toes. Provide tempera paint poured over a folded paper towel to create a stamp pad. Use the turkey foot as a stamp and print footprints over the letters in turkey.

Home Connection

○ Suggest that children show their families how to do a "Hootchy-Kootchy Dance."

I've Been Workin' on the Railroad

I've been workin' on the railroad
All the live long day.
I've been workin' on the railroad,
Just to pass the time away.
Don't you hear the whistle blowing?
Rise up so early in the morn.
Don't you hear the captain shouting?
Dinah, blow your horn.

Dinah, won't you blow, Dinah, won't you blow,
Dinah, won't you blow your horn, your horn?
Dinah, won't you blow, Dinah, won't you blow,
Dinah, won't you blow your horn?

Someone's in the kitchen with Dinah.
Someone's in the kitchen, I know.
Someone's in the kitchen with Dinah
Strumming on the old banjo.

Fee, fie, fiddle-e-i-o.
Fee, fie, fiddle-e-i-o.
Fee, fie, fiddle-e-i-o.
Strumming on the old banjo.

Vocabulary

banjo
captain
kitchen
live long
pass
railroad
strum
whistle

Theme Connections

Music
Sounds
Transportation
Workers

Did You Know?

○ The origins of this song are unknown. Some trace it back to a "Louisiana Levee" song of African-Americans. Others believe it is an old hymn adapted by the Irish work gangs in the West. The verses that begin with "Dinah" and "Someone's in the Kitchen" are later additions.

○ This tune was adapted by Texans as *The Eyes of Texas Are Upon You*. The horn signifies the call to lunch.

○ "The Eyes of Texas" is the official song of the University of Texas. It was written in 1903 by John Sinclair for the Cowboy Minstrel Show. Mr. Sinclair used a famous saying of Colonel Prather, who was the President of the University. The Colonel always told his audiences to remember that "the eyes of Texas are upon you," so Mr. Sinclair fit this saying to the tune of "I've Been Working on the Railroad."

Literacy Links

Comprehension

○ Show children road signs. Call their attention to the sign for railroad crossing.

（✓） **Special Needs Adaptation:** This activity provides an opportunity to teach other road signs as well. Show the children road signs and call their attention to the railroad crossing sign. In addition, select a few other common road signs such as "stop," "caution," or "yield." Talk about the meaning of each sign. Use this lesson to reinforce typical safety rules, such as looking before you cross the street, never walking or playing near railroad tracks, and never trying to cross a railroad track when the gate is down.

Oral Language

○ Discuss working on the railroad. *What jobs do people do?*

Phonological Awareness

○ Print *fee, fie, fiddle-e-i-o* on chart paper. Discuss the repetition of the letter "f" in the first three words. Read the phrase and have the children repeat it. Mention that the repetitive sounds of the first letter in the words is called *alliteration*. Substitute another letter for the letter "f" and say the phrase again. For example, use a "t" to change the phrase to "tee, tie, tiddle-e-i-o." Continue changing the letter for as long as the children are interested.

○ Invite children to think of words that rhyme with fiddle.

Curriculum Connections

Blocks

○ Build a train track with blocks. Provide a train and encourage the children to run the train over the tracks. Add signs along the track; for example, railroad crossing, station signs, and town signs.

Dramatic Play

○ Set up a train station. Provide tickets, conductor hats, serving trays, and chairs for train seats. Invite the children to pretend they are riding the train.

Book Corner

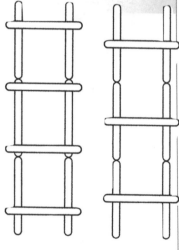

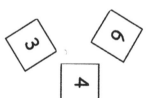

Field Trip
❍ Visit a train station. Point out the location of ticket agents, platforms, terminals and so on.

Fine Motor
❍ Provide masking tape. Invite the children to make a masking tape train track on a table top.

Games
❍ Select a child to be the engine. Have the group recite the rhyme below. At the end of each verse have the engine select another car.

Listening
❍ Provide horns and whistles for the children to explore; for example, bicycle horns, party horns, train whistles. Provide empty toilet paper tubes and crayons for the children to use to make a horn of their own.

Math
❍ Make railroad tracks by gluing craft sticks together. Make a track with three crossties, four crossties, five crossties, six crossties, and so on up to ten crossties. Prepare numeral cards 3-10. Invite the children to match the tracks according to the number of crossties to the correct numeral card.

Snack
❍ Invite the children to make train tracks with pretzels. Use long and short pretzels to make the tracks.

> Little red train,
> Chugging down the track.
> First it goes down,
> Then it comes back,
> Hooking on cars one by one.

Writing
❍ Draw a railroad crossing sign and encourage children to copy the sign.

Home Connection

❍ Suggest that families visit a railroad station. Encourage them to take a look at the train tracks, ticket windows, train cars, schedules, train platforms, and so on.

More Learning and Fun

Songs

The Arkansas Traveler

Oh, once upon a time in Arkansas,
An old man sat in his little cabin door
And fiddled at a tune that he liked to hear,
A jolly old tune that he played by ear.
It was raining hard, but the fiddler didn't care,
He sawed away at the popular air,
Tho' his rooftree leaked like a waterfall,
That didn't seem to bother the man at all.

Old Chisholm Trail

Well, come along, boys and listen to my tale,
I'll tell you of my troubles on the old
    Chisholm Trail,
Come a ti, yi, yippi-yappi, yay, yappi, yay,
Come a ti, yi, yippi-yappi, yay.

Two-dollar hoss and a forty-dollar saddle,
And I'm goin' to punchin' those Texas cattle.
Come a ti, yi, yippi-yappi, yay, yappi, yay,
Come a ti, yi, yippi-yappi, yay.

I can ride any hoss in the wild and woolly West,
I can ride him, I can rope him, I can make him
    do his best.
Come a ti, yi, yippi-yappi, yay, yappi, yay,
Come a ti, yi, yippi-yappi, yay.

O, it's bacon and beans 'most every day,
I'd as soon be a-eatin' prairie hay.
Come a ti, yi, yippi-yappi, yay, yappi, yay,
Come a ti, yi, yippi-yappi, yay.

Ragtime Cowboy Joe

Out in Arizona where the bad men are,
And the only friend to guide you is an
    evening star,
The roughest, toughest man by far is Ragtime
    Cowboy Joe.
Got his name from singing to the cows and sheep
Every night they say he sings the herd to sleep
In a basso rich and deep, crooning soft and low.

How he sings, raggy music to his cattle
As he swings back and forward in his saddle
On his horse (a pretty good horse), who is
    a syncopated gaiter,
And with such a funny meter to the roar of
    his repeater.

Poems

Shoo-Fly Pie

Shoo-fly pie
And apple pan dowdy
Make your eyes light up
And your stomach say "howdy."

Shoo-fly pie
And apple pan dowdy
I never get enough
Of that wonderful stuff.

Fingerplays

I'm a Little Cowboy/Cowgirl

I'm a little cowboy/cowgirl. Here's my hat. *(point to hat)*
Here are my spurs and here are my chaps. *(point to feet and legs)*
When I get up, I work all day, *(jump)*
Get on my horse and ride away. *(gallop away)*

I Hop on My Horse

I hop on my horse and off I go *(pretend to hop on horse)*
"Giddy up, Baby, and don't be slow."
    (pretend shake the reins)
The sun blazes hot. The sandy winds blow.
    (put hands on head and face)
But Baby keeps going 'til I say, "Whoa!"
    (pretend to pull back on reins)

Action Story

Going on a Trail Ride by Pam Schiller

(The children echo you after each line. Suit actions to the words.)
We're going on a trail ride.
Want to come along?
Well, then, come on.
Let's get ready!

Got to rope and brand the cattle.
Let's rope.
Stick on the brand.
Got to load up the chuck wagon.
Get the blankets and the food.
Don't forget the water.
Got to water our horses.
Slurp, slurp.
Ready to go.

Now jump on your horse.
Let's go.

(Children pretend to hold horse reins and clip clop between all verses.)

Look! There's a river.
Can't go over it.
Can't go under it.
Can't go around it.
We'll have to go through it. *(hold the reins and make a sloshing sound)*

Look! There's some cactus.
Can't go under it.
Can't go over it.
Can't go through it.
We'll have to go around it. *(lean left and clip clop)*

Look! There's a mountain.
Can't go through it.
Can't go under it.
Can't go around it.
We'll have to go over it. *(lean back)*

Look! There's a wagon train.
Can't go through it.
Can't go under it.
Can't go over it.
We'll have to go around it.

Look! There's the town!
Just what we are looking for!
Let's hurry! Get along, little dogies! *(ride fast)*
We're almost there. *(continue to ride fast)*
Civilization at last!

Listening Story

Quinn and Dusty

(Have the children call out yippee every time you say Quinn and call out giddy-up every time you say Dusty.)

Quinn and Dusty rode into the corral. They were tired. They had had a full day of riding the herd. Quinn was moving his cattle to a new grazing place.

Quinn pulled back on the reins, and Dusty stopped abruptly. He dismounted. He untied the saddle and lifted it from Dusty's back. Dusty shook with relief and neighed. He was plain out of giddy-up. (That's why you are giving him yours.)

Quinn put the saddle and blanket in their place in the tack room. He picked up the currycomb and began combing Dusty's mane. If Dusty could have purred like a pleased kitten he would have. But he was too tired to do anything but close his eyes and enjoy the gentle scratching on his body.

Quinn finished combing his friend and put the currycomb away. He filled a pail with water and emptied it into Dusty's trough. He shoveled up a load of hay and dumped it at Dusty's feet.

He gave Dusty's neck a rub, turned out the light and headed for the ranch house. He was ready for his own "getting ready for bed routine."

Quinn opened the door to the house. He could smell the cowboy stew his wife had fixed for dinner. His stomach growled in anticipation.

Quinn pulled off his boots and placed them by the door. He took off his hat and heavy vest and hung them on the hook above his boots. He shook himself with relief. He was so tired, he was out of yippee. (That's why you are giving him yours.)

Quinn and Dusty both slept well. They dreamed of the green tall grass prairie, the warmth of the sun, the smell of the earth, and the occasional stray cow needing to be herded. And so ends the story of Quinn and Dusty.

Fun Facts Related to Wild, Wild West

Cowboys

○ Spanish cattle were first brought to New Spain (Mexico) in the early 1500s. Gradually, as the Spaniards pushed northward into what is now the Southwestern United States, they brought their cattle to establish ranches in "Tejas." When Mexico won its independence from Spain in 1821, many settlers left their herds of Longhorn cattle behind. The catttle prospered and multiplied in the wild grasslands.

○ Just before the Mexican Revolution, Moses Austin received approval for American colonists to settle in this part of Mexico and immigrants began to pour into the area. These newcomers discovered the wild cattle roaming Tejas. This was a resource too good to believe, and some of the early settlers learned from the Mexicans and Indians how to rope the longhorns from horseback.

○ There was no transportation in early Texas; no way to move products to faraway markets. It didn't take long to figure out that cattle were the only product around that provided their own transportation to market! By the 1830s, the trade in Texas cattle was booming and providing prosperity to the immigrants. The first Texas trail drives were short trips, but when short routes became unprofitable, the long trail rides began.

Recipes

Cowboy Stew

Place slices of finely diced onion, potatoes, carrots, and beans in beef bouillon in a crock pot. Add ground beef meatballs (mix together egg, bread crumbs, and ground beef). Season with garlic, salt, and pepper. Cook until the meatballs are completely cooked and the vegetables are tender.

Snicker Doodles

2 ¾ cups sifted flour
1 teaspoon baking soda
2 teaspoons cream of tartar
¼ teaspoon salt
1 cup shortening
1 ¾ cup sugar, divided
2 eggs
1 teaspoon vanilla
1 tablespoon cinnamon

Sift together flour, soda, cream of tartar and salt. Cream shortening and 1 ½ cups sugar. Add eggs and vanilla. Add dry ingredients and blend well. Chill dough until easy to handle. Combine ¼ cup sugar and cinnamon. Roll dough into balls and dip into sugar-cinnamon mixture. Bake at 350° on greased cookie sheet for 10-15 minutes. Makes 4 or 5 dozen.

Brand Patterns

Clown Rhyming Word Cards

down

Rose Rhyming Word Cards

Western Duds Patterns

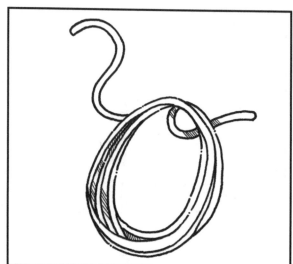
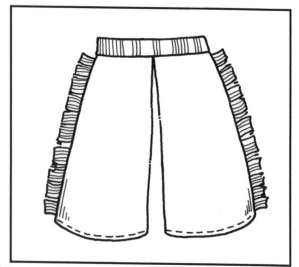
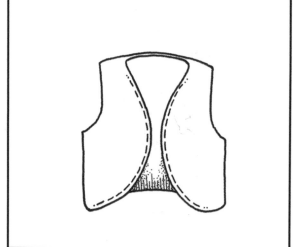

Western Patterns

Western Patterns

Buckaroo Cookie Rebus Recipe

Buckaroo Cookies

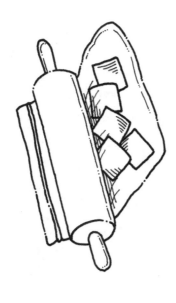

Put six graham crackers in a re-sealable bag and crush them with a rolling pin.

Roll into balls and then eat!

1/2 cup raisins

1/2 cup chopped dates

2 tablespoons of honey

Mix the raisins, chopped dates and honey in a mixing bowl.

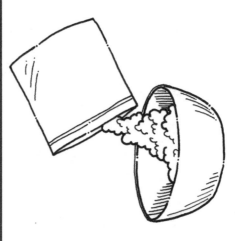

Add crushed crackers to the other mixture until it is dry enough to roll into balls.

Haystack Rebus Recipe

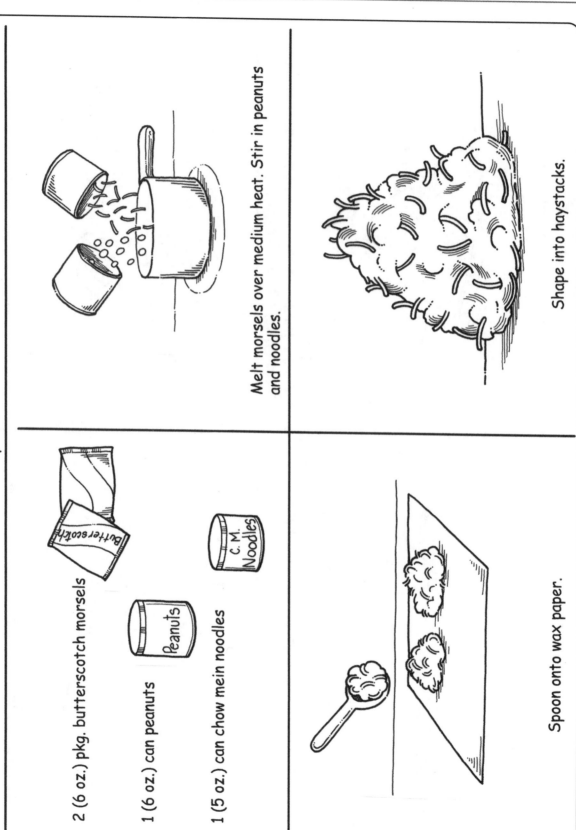

Haystacks

2 (6 oz.) pkg. butterscotch morsels

1 (6 oz.) can peanuts

1 (5 oz.) can chow mein noodles

Melt morsels over medium heat. Stir in peanuts and noodles.

Shape into haystacks.

Spoon onto wax paper.

Horsie Cookie Rebus Recipe

Horsie Cookie

Provide wafer cookie for a base.

Spread peanut butter on the cookie.

Stand a horse cookie on top.

Eat and enjoy!

Oodles Noodles Rebus Recipe

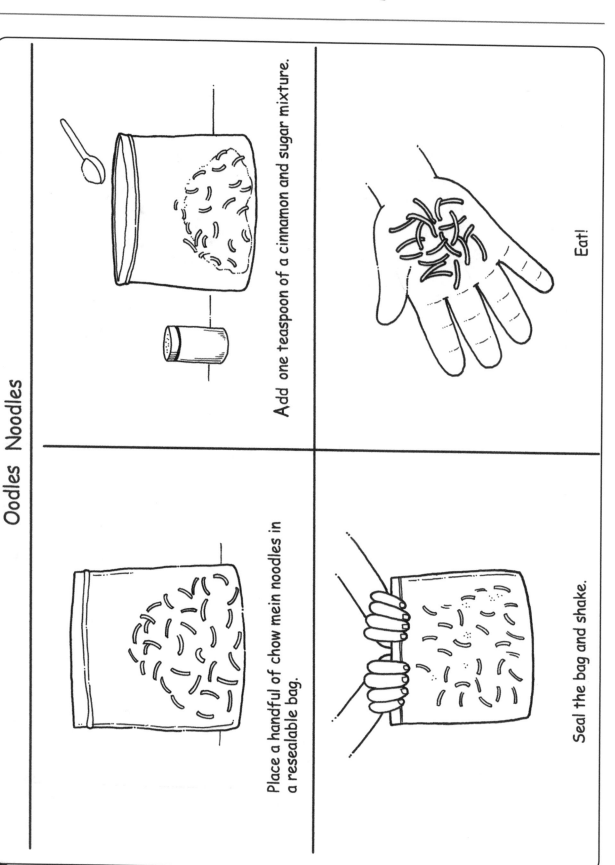

Oodles Noodles

Add one teaspoon of a cinnamon and sugar mixture.

Eat!

Place a handful of chow mein noodles in a resealable bag.

Seal the bag and shake.

Prairie Home Rebus Recipe

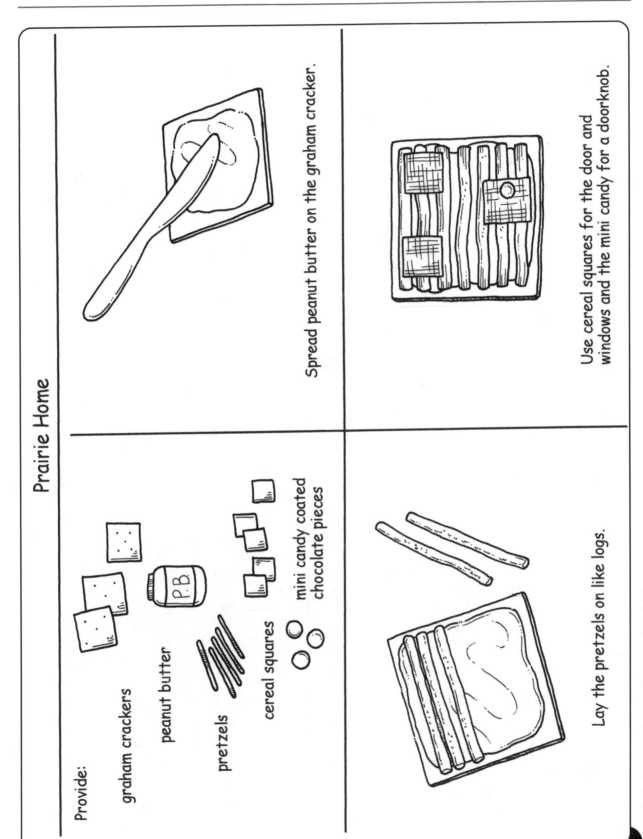

Prairie Home

Provide:

graham crackers

peanut butter

pretzels

cereal squares

mini candy coated chocolate pieces

Spread peanut butter on the graham cracker.

Use cereal squares for the door and windows and the mini candy for a doorknob.

Lay the pretzels on like logs.

Smiling Pizza Face Rebus Recipe

Smiling Pizza Face

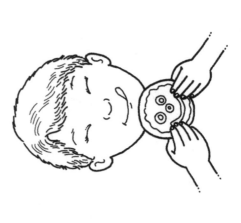

Have the children brush on pizza sauce and then cover their muffin with pizza cheese.

Heat and eat!

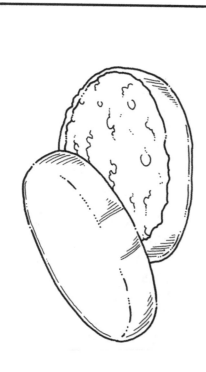

Give each child one-half of an english muffin.

Provide olives and pepperoni sausages for the eyes and nose and slices of red bell peppers for the mouth.

Trail Mix Rebus Recipe

Trail Mix

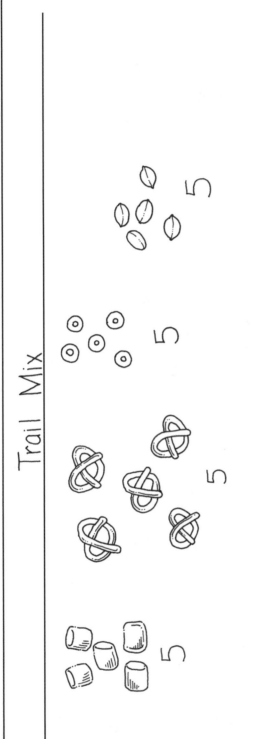

5
5
5
5
5

Count 5 marshmallows, 5 pretzels, 5 pieces of cereal, and 5 peanuts.

Put into a plastic cup.

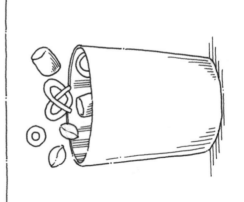

Enjoy!

American Sign Language Signs

Cowboy

Home

Cow/Cattle

Hat

Goodbye

Boots

Girl

American Sign Language Signs

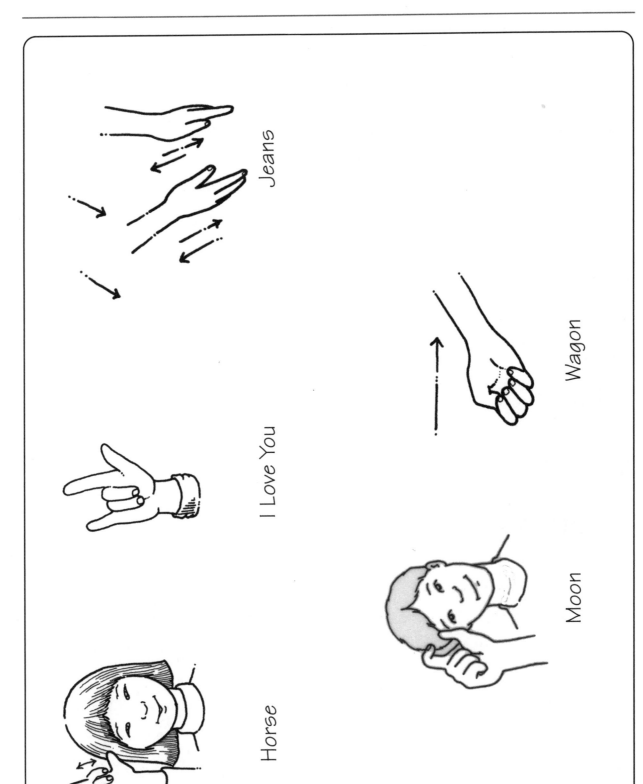

Jeans

Wagon

I Love You

Moon

Horse

References and Bibliography

Bulloch, Kathleen. 2003. *The mystery of modifying: Creative solutions.* Education Service Center, Region VI: Huntsville, Texas.

Cavallaro, C. & M. Haney. 1999. *Preschool inclusion.* Paul H. Brookes Publishing Co: Baltimore, MD.

Gray, T. & S. Fleischman. "Research Matters; Successful Strategies for English Language Learners." *Educational Leadership,* Dec. 2004-Jan. 2005, Volume 62, 84-85.

Hanniford, Carla. 1995. *Smart moves: Why learning is not all in your head.* Great Ocean Publications: Arlington, Virginia, p. 146.

Keller, M. 2004. "Warm weather boosts mood, broadens the mind." *Post Doctoral Study: The University of Michigan,* Ann Arbor, MI.

LeDoux, Joseph. (1993). "Emotional memory systems in the brain." *Behavioral and Brain Research,* vol 58.

Theme Index

Children's Book Index

Index